God Bumps

By Gail Withey

God Bumps

Copyright 2023 by Gail Withey

Hardback ISBN # 979-8-9924578-4-1

Paperback ISBN # 979-8-9924578-5-8

Ebook ISBN # 979-8-9924578-3-4

**Published by Smoky Water Press
PO Box 2322, Bismarck, ND 58502**

**Purchase online at
www.DakotaBookNet.com**

Cover design and art by Linda Donlin

God Bumps

*Everyday People
Sharing Inspirational
Stories About the
Tremendous Impact of God's Grace*

By Gail Withey

Contents

Dedication

Though my parents are in Heaven with our Lord, it was they who taught me how to be strong and never give up.

To my lovely mother, Isabell, who always believed in me and encouraged me to follow my dreams. Her love and support have meant everything to me. I am blessed and grateful to have had you as my mother and my friend.

To my amazing father, Robert, who was always there for me. I am ever so grateful for the wisdom, strength, and endless love I had in the father I was blessed with. I am thankful to have had you as my father and my friend.

Gail Withey

I was born and raised in Willow City in northern North Dakota, where the population was sparse and everyone knew each other. The school I attended had grades 1 through 5 and 7 through 12 in the same building. Grade 6 was across a gravel street in a true one-room schoolhouse. It had been updated with running water and electricity, but the the original real blackboard and hardwood floors were still there.

When I was 13, my parents opened a mom-and-pop eatery, and I worked there. That business sold after I graduated from high school, but I continued to cook for 36 years, including running my own catering company.

At a young age, I loved to write poetry and song lyrics and taught myself to play piano. I played and sang in my church, growing closer to God through that ministry and helping others grow closer to God as well. I've always been a storyteller, studied communications in college and worked as a newspaper correspondent and newsletter editor. My philosophy is that everyone has a story.

In 2010 I published a children's book called *Give It Up*, and recorded a CD with Christian songs that I wrote. Unfortunately, the publishing company went out of business, and I suffered some losses as a result. But that hasn't deterred me from pursuing my passion for giving others hope through the written word.

One day I was listening to Real Presence radio and heard a local woman sharing her story about the Lord's impact on her life. I called her, and the idea for *God Bumps*, was born – a collection of stories told by real people about their extraordinary encounters with the Lord. Jesus was the ultimate storyteller, so I decided to collect 33 stories that would help personify His message and keep it alive and well.

Visiting with people and gathering their amazing stories has been a divine journey. It took longer than I expected, but the experience was worthwhile and has strengthened my faith. Their stories are inspirational, and I thank each one for sharing them. I have other works in the pipeline that support my passion for helping draw people closer to God, and I am excited for what the future holds.

Foreword

I first met Gail Withey when she worked in activities at the assisted living facility where my mom was a resident. She loved Gail, and our paths crossed often while Mom lived there. Mom was honored when Gail wrote a newsletter story about her. Because I was a professional writer and editor, Mom asked me to look at the story and offer suggestions. Not long after that, Mom passed away, and Gail moved on. We lost touch, except for seeing each other in church occasionally.

One Sunday, Gail approached me about editing a prayer guide she was writing. She had a great deal of experience with different types of writing: for business, as a journalist, and she had previously published a Christian children's book. She remembered my background as an editor and asked me to look at her project. I was happy to help review it.

Through working on that prayer guide, we started a professional relationship that turned into a friendship. Soon we began talking about this book, *God Bumps*, and Gail's vision for it. I was intrigued with the concept and impressed with Gail's steadfast faith and with her ability to encourage people to share their personal stories about their experiences. I agreed to help edit them, and as each story came in, I grew more excited about the potential for Gail's book. I believed in it so much that I decided to add my own story to the list!

In *God Bumps,* 33 everyday people share their amazing, true stories of their life-changing encounters with God's grace. Some stories will slightly raise the hair on the back of your neck; others will shake you to the depths of your soul. You've heard of and likely experienced goosebumps in your life. After reading this book, you will know what God Bumps are! You will also know without a doubt that, with God, anything is possible.

Linda Donlin

Chapter 1

Native Son Turns to God

"God heard my prayers and baptized me in the Holy Spirit. It was the most indescribable feeling, something I'd never experienced before."

32. Thirty-two years on drugs. 32.

How did I survive that and live to talk about it? And not just live to talk about it: but live to testify about it. To testify that my survival was only possible because God had a plan for me. That the Holy Ghost came into my soul and gurgled out through my being in God Bumps that set me in the right direction.

My name is Chad. I was born in 1977 and spent my early years on a reservation in North Dakota with my parents and six brothers and sisters. My dad worked as a journeyman brick mason, and his job required him to travel quite a bit. Mom was a homemaker, but she would occasionally take part-time jobs when money was tight. When Dad was home, he was strict, and seemed harder on me as the oldest.

Our home life was mostly loving, but we did come from a family of heavy drinkers and drug abusers. I was very close to my grandfather, who was my biggest fan. I

1

started playing sports and found my niche in football and basketball. All my friends were on the team. Life was good.

My father had been bouncing around from company to company in the union, but he found a job in Minnesota. He did well there and was hired as a foreman for the union. It was stable. When I was 11, the decision was made to move our family to Minnesota, so that we could all be together. I didn't want to move. My parents knew that and allowed me to stay back with my grandparents for the summer.

When I did start school in Minnesota, things went well at first. I excelled in football and basketball. After the season ended, there were tryouts for the Amateur Athletics Union's basketball summer program. I was the top player on our team and was first picked for the opportunity to go to AAU. But money was an issue. We couldn't afford it. I was disappointed, but the coach said they'd be in touch.

One day, the phone rang. It was the AAU assistant coach, offering me a scholarship. There were important practices coming up, and he said they needed me to be there. Our family already had plans to go back to North Dakota for the weekend, but the coach said I could stay with them. I was thrilled!

The assistant coach and his wife picked me up, and we went to lunch, and then back to their place. I shot hoops all day, and then got called in to clean up for dinner. This family prayed fervently at meals, and I thought they really believed in God. I tried to be on my best behavior.

That night, the assistant coach came into my room. I felt his elbow on the back of my neck. He had a tiny club, and started hitting me with it, calling me derogatory names. Then he raped me. Over and over. For five or six hours. I saw his wife standing at the door. She knew what was going on. How could they do this to an 11-year-old boy?

The abuse continued for the next two to three nights. I was supposed to be at practice, but he told the head coach I was sick. I was bruised all over. He said my behavior wasn't good, and I didn't want to play in the last two games. I went to the games and sat on the end of the bench, crying my heart out. My dad couldn't believe it. He asked me how I went from being the best player on the team to not playing at all. He asked me what was wrong, but I was scared to tell him. I believed that the assistant coach had money, and money bought everything. Including my innocence.

From then on, I was afraid of everything and everyone. I trusted no one. I was even afraid in my parents' apartment. I hid my feelings by playing video games all the time. I became a loner; I was scared to be around people by myself. Everyone knew I had changed, that something must have happened, but no one could figure it out. And I couldn't bring myself to tell anyone.

One day a friend at school handed me a little packet

of tin foil. His big brother was a drug dealer, and he said this would take care of all of Chad's problems. I carried it around for about a month. I felt myself slowly going down into a deep depression over the abuse, so I decided to give it a try. I felt everything go numb as the drugs entered my body. The addiction was instant. I was 12.

By the age of 15, I was an expert drug dealer. Whatever I made in profit, I used to buy drugs for myself. I had all that abuse inside of me that I was trying to block out. By 16, the drugs were no longer working on my depression, which had now turned to anger. I was having nightmares, and the abuse haunted me daily. I went to see my dealer one day and saw a gun on the table. I asked the price, and I couldn't afford it. I told him what had happened to me and that I wanted to kill the assistant coach. He handed me the gun with a full clip.

I took it to school two days later and put it in my gym locker. Someone saw it and reported me. A security guard grabbed me and took the gun. Eventually I was expelled. One of my coaches told my parents I was a good kid, and he knew I was struggling with something. He said I needed counseling, not prison. I went to four high schools in four years.

I got into boxing and wrestling, which helped somewhat, as it was a positive, physical way to vent my anger. But unfortunately, I started getting in fights outside of school. By the time I was 17, I was fighting men in their 20s and 30s. I have scars all over, was stabbed in a bar fight and shot over a drug deal gone wrong. I started having thoughts about taking my own life.

I spent most of my adult life homeless, suicidal, and bouncing in and out of treatment facilities. I got married when I was 27 and straightened up for a while. I found a job and started being responsible. But my marriage ended in divorce, and about that time I found out that my co-workers were using drugs. I started again, and soon I lost my job and my car. I wandered around homeless, sleeping down by the river, spending my days trying to figure out how to eat and pay for drugs. I felt as if I was losing my mind.

I hit rock bottom in 2016 and formulated a plan to kill myself. I slit my arms from wrist to elbow, crawled up in a tree and attempted to hang myself with a jump rope. I passed out, but I remember the dream I had. Or maybe it wasn't a dream. I saw myself in my hometown church with my youngest son and daughter. I felt water coming up all over, and I saw my son reaching for me, urging me to get out. But the water caught fire; it turned into a lake of fire. I believe I was actually in hell; there were people drowning and suffering all around. It was terrifying!

Suddenly there were lights all around, and a light came closer and closer to me. It grabbed my arm and pulled me out above all the suffering people. I heard my name being called. "Chad, Chad, you are not done yet. I'm not finished with you." I saw an outline of a body, but no one was there. I saw lights shooting off my arms, and then everything went black, except for the light of the moon. I woke up at 6 a.m., feeling like someone was standing in the sun above me, urging me to get up, but no one was there. I looked around and saw dried blood everywhere. The deep gashes I had made in my arms had already started to heal, now appearing only as dots. I washed the blood off with a bottle of water, put on my hoodie, grabbed my backpack, and went to a gas station to clean up. I saw a church across the street and remembered that I had a friend who played in the worship band there. I went to the church and heard the words I needed to hear: "Trust that God will provide. It's all about faith. Take one step at a time."

Something had changed within me. In the next two weeks, I got a job as a mason and an apartment. A friend gave me a car, and I went straight to Alcoholics Anonymous. At a meeting, I heard about another church and decided to go there. A man gave testimony that day about how he had felt alone, lost in his own head, and unforgiveable. He said he kept hearing these words: "There's no place in the kingdom of Heaven for people like me."

I suddenly realized that's what I used to tell myself when people talked about God. I would hear that assistant coach's voice in my head, telling me that I was a mistake, and that God didn't love people like me. I needed to hear that testimony that day because I knew something special had happened to this man, and to me. It was two weeks after I had tried to commit suicide, and I knew without a doubt that God had saved my life. I realized that God had His hand in my life all this time. He does love me, and there is a purpose for my life.

But still I went back and forth with my faith. I came into it with a childlike mentality, so I had to learn everything new. My friend told me I needed to dive into God to truly know Him. I prayed for love and acceptance, and I found that in my church family. Eventually I stopped believing the lies I had been told, and I started forgiving myself. I was gradually breaking free from the prison that I had been locked in. I was taking baby steps to full surrender; God was giving me a new heart.

On November 11, 2018, a childhood friend committed suicide. It was very difficult for me to accept. I prayed fervently for the gift of knowledge, of understanding. God heard my prayers and baptized me in the Holy Spirit. It was the most indescribable feeling, something I'd never experienced before. God Bumps for sure! I was on a different kind of high for at least two weeks.

One day my pastor approached me about a radio station they had at the church that hadn't been used for years. He asked me if I wanted to manage it. I had never done anything like that before; I didn't even know what a sound board was. But within five months, I had learned how everything works and was talking to people about my experiences.

My faith was growing, but I struggled every day to keep on the right path. My good friend at church, the one who drew me in with his testimony, and I would often talk about being "all in," about trying to help others. He became gravely ill, and as I visited him on his deathbed, we talked about my becoming a pastor. But his passing really shook me up, and I pulled away from that idea. I was pallbearer at his funeral, and people talked about how he had positively impacted their lives. They said someone needed to fill his shoes. I just put my head down and didn't say anything. I ran from my calling for more than a year.

I still suffered from PTSD from the abuse. I opened the paper one day, intending to look for the sports page. Instead, I turned to the death notices, and there was the obituary for my abuser. It was a shock, but it also was a moment of reckoning. I realized that God healed me from having thoughts about wanting to hurt pedophiles. I now feel sorry for them. I want to spend my life teaching people how to recognize the signs of abuse and helping those who have been abused.

My goal now is to help people, as I have been helped. I want to bring God into places like reservations. There is so much generational trauma; I want to show them that God can meet them where they are. I want to find as many strong Christian Native Americans as I can to help the children, to get them involved in positive activities. I ran into a younger version of myself recently, someone who didn't trust anyone in authority, and I was able to relate to him. I recognize that I have a gift to connect with youth, to help them find God. I want to help them see that God has a plan, and they are not alone.

The dream that my friend and I talked about on his deathbed was to open a "one-stop healing shop" that would have a homeless shelter, food bank, treatment facility, transitional living community and a church. I'm finishing my degree in Behavioral Health and want to open a center for addicts that will provide recovery services and help them with securing employment, sober living, peer support and mentors so that they are in a place mentally and physically, as well as spiritually to succeed. It's the fulfillment of that dream. I am definitely "all in." I don't know if I can ever fill his shoes, but I'm sure going to try to help as many people as I can.

If I've learned anything in my faith journey, it's that with God, anything is possible. He pulled me from the abyss and set me on the right path. I depend on God daily, and He gives me guidance. His love saved me, and He did it for a reason. The God Bumps that came rushing through me have turned into a passion for helping others who need God as much as I did, and still do. Together, we will find the key to salvation.

Chad Davis

Chapter 2

Jesus, I Trust in You

*"It was a God Bump moment when I realized that
in one of my darkest hours, this time of hope
and waiting was destined to be my Advent journey."*

God Bumps are clear messages from the Holy Spirit - those
times when the hair on your arm stands up or when you
get goosebumps, but you aren't cold - this is the work of
the Holy Spirit. This work has allowed me to experience
God Bumps in some of my darkest moments, and also in
some of my most joyous moments.

The first experience of God Bumps came in 1994 as I
heard our daughter Hailey cry in the NICU the day she
was born. Sixteen weeks into our first pregnancy, doctors
discovered our baby girl would be born with Spina Bifida.
She only had a 10 percent chance of surviving. The doctors
prepared us to expect that her head could be the size of
a basketball or that she could have a foot growing out
the side of her leg. So, hearing her cry and seeing how
beautiful she was despite having Spina Bifida, was a joyful
God Bump moment.

Despite the predictions, Hailey led a fairly normal life. But
when she was 20, she was scheduled to have a colostomy at
the University of Minnesota. Knowing Hailey was going to

be in surgery for a while, I wanted to be prepared with a good book. I picked up a book about Advent, but I had no idea what a gift from God it would turn out to be.

The book included scripture readings, meditations, words of encouragement and prayers. The author suggested carving out a few moments daily to embrace the gift of Christmas through reflections, worship and prayer. She said there was a good chance something new would be born in my heart, so when Christmas Day arrived, I would be able to truly celebrate what God has done and what He promised to do.

It was the night before the first Sunday of Advent, and Hailey was having a hard time keeping her oxygen levels to where they should be. As the hours passed, her oxygen levels kept dropping. She needed to go to the ICU. The doctor told us that her lungs were extremely sick, and she would need to be put into a coma. All we could do as parents at this point was WAIT. It was a God Bump moment when I realized that in one of my darkest hours, this time of hope and waiting was destined to be my Advent journey.

The first reflection that I read was from Lamentations 3:26, which says that it's good to wait quietly for the salvation of the Lord. But we don't like to wait because it feels like it's a waste of time. But what I read is that we need to trust in how God is orchestrating everything behind the scenes while we are waiting. The prayer for the day focused on opening our hearts and hands to God's purposes and plans while we are waiting. It asked that I be blessed with patience and that I believed God was working on my daughter's behalf at this moment.

As the days became weeks, I shared my faith with each nurse and doctor who cared for Hailey, but her health was deteriorating. Each time they needed to move Hailey into a different position, she would code, and they would have to bag her for a few minutes. The doctor said that if she got any worse, they would have to do one more procedure, placing Hailey on an ECMO (Extracorporeal membrane oxygenation) machine. This machine drains the blood from the veins, adds oxygen and removes carbon dioxide. It then returns it to the veins and pumps the blood throughout the body. The ECMO machine allows the blood to bypass the heart and lungs.

At this point, all we could do was to wait, hope, pray and trust. December 6th was the day Hailey was placed on the ECMO. We needed to sign papers allowing them to do this procedure. My signature was as follows: Melody Haider, Jesus I Trust in You.

Through my tears, I continued to read my book. The prayer this day was about being in the middle of a storm or when facing the most formidable enemies, that we must set our hopes on Jesus to fight for us. The reflection was that God doesn't blink at roadblocks – after all, He parted the Red Sea. He can part any stormy sea in our lives. This was a God Bump moment for me. I felt these words were written just for me. Another reflection dealt with God keeping his promise. No matter the circumstance, He is reaching out to us, even if we are falling.

As days went by, Hailey lost a lot of blood because they needed to keep her blood thin so it could pass through the machine. Early one morning, the doctor called, telling us to come to the hospital. Because of the bleeding, they needed to replace her chest tube with a larger one. Again, this was a critical moment. All we could do was to hope in the Lord. God Bumps came on strongly when she made it through this procedure.

A few days later, we learned that because of the blood loss, Hailey would need to come off the ECMO whether she was ready or not. God Bumps appeared when her numbers improved overnight, and they felt confident that she was ready to be taken off. By God's Grace, the procedure went well.

I turned to my book, and the reflection prayer was one of thankfulness: being thankful for what God has so freely given us. One of the passages dealt with the fact that what we are waiting for is no more important than who we become while waiting. There was so much truth in that. I was truly transforming into who God wanted me to become during this Advent season.

Christmas was getting closer, and our hope was gradually getting stronger. Hailey was still on the ventilator but was improving each day. On December 23, the doctor was in Hailey's room, making adjustments to the machines she was on. He turned the ventilator off to see if Hailey could breathe on her own. By God's Grace, she did! God Bumps came as we saw she was breathing on her own, even though she tired easily. God Bumps were back when the doctor declared Hailey was our Christmas miracle and would be taken off the machines the next morning: Christmas Eve. Our family and the staff at the hospital clearly saw that this was our Advent Journey of hope and waiting, and it was no accident that God clearly led me through this beautiful, yet scary, Advent.

The last prayer I prayed from my Advent book as I sat at Midnight Mass was a reflection on stillness, knowing that God was near, and He is all we need. It talked about the unconditional love of sending His son to us and that we must trust Him with our present and our future.

It was a Silent Night, a Holy Night, all was calm, all was bright as we stood around Hailey's bed giving God thanks for the Miracle that only He could do as we waited through this Advent season.

Hailey continued with rehab at the University of Minnesota for two weeks and then came home. She continues to do well and is working. She recently got married, and there wasn't a dry eye in the church as she walked down the aisle. Those who witnessed our God Bumps and the Advent Journey marveled with us that it ended so beautifully. We pray that all those who read this will come away with hope and trust in the journey that God has planned for each of them.

Melody Haider

Chapter 3

God Bump Visions Bring Peace

"The Good Lord has his ways of shocking us, of letting us know that we're only here for a little while."

In 2013, I started feeling ill. I doctored in Bismarck for about a year, and then went to Mayo Clinic. There, I was diagnosed with Stage 4 Non-Hodgkin's Lymphoma. The doctors started me on a course of six treatments, the first of which I had at Mayo. I was then scheduled to take the rest of the treatments in Bismarck.

I progressively got weaker from the treatments and from the cancer, which had spread throughout my entire body. I was so ill that the doctors decided to delay my fifth treatment. I was in a great deal of pain, and I slept in a different room from my wife so that we could both try to get some rest.

One night I woke up, and my wife could hear me talking. She heard me say that if I died the next minute, I was okay with that. What she didn't know was that I was having a vision.

I saw four or five individuals, all different heights and

completely white, at the foot of my bed. They had no faces and moved slowly around me. I probably should have been scared, but I wasn't. I was wide awake, and I had this overwhelming feeling of peace. I did get frustrated because I was asking them questions, and they wouldn't talk to me. But I still felt at peace. That was the first God Bump on my journey.

During my treatment, my father was in a nursing home, suffering from dementia. My mother had passed away five years earlier. One evening I went to visit him, and he couldn't talk to me. I sat with him, and suddenly Mom appeared to us. She told Dad he wasn't ready to go, but that she would come get him when it was his time. He responded to her and then was quiet. After that, when he did talk, he was as clear as a bell. The morning he passed, I knew it instantly by the feeling that came over me. Sure enough, I got a call 15 minutes later with that news. I was sad, but relieved, as I knew he was now at peace – and with Mom. That was the next God Bump.

A few weeks after Dad's funeral, I saw him one night. He appeared in a cross and told me I didn't have to pray for my healing, that I was going to be okay. My wife asked me the next morning who I was talking to, and I described my vision. She said, "I don't know what you saw, but I didn't see anything." But I knew I had clearly seen and heard him. God Bump!

Not long after that, I had my sixth treatment in Bismarck. When I woke up, I could feel the cancer being pulled out of me. I could actually feel it leaving my body. Before that I was in constant pain, but after that happened, the pain disappeared.

When my wife came to get me, I told her the cancer was gone. I said, "I don't know if it was the angels or what, but the cancer has been pulled out of me." I felt great; I was still weak, but I felt this overwhelming sense of relief. It was hard to hold back tears. My wife believed me, and we rejoiced together. She said she never questioned me about anything that happened on this journey. We knew that I wasn't ready to go; there's a purpose for me yet in this life. God Bump!

More than five years later, I am still cancer free. One of my oncologists told me that he didn't have much hope when he reviewed my case. He believes my recovery was a miracle. God Bump!

After going through all this, I learned that I am ready to go any time. The Good Lord has his ways of shocking us, of letting us know that we're only here for a little while. We must appreciate our time on earth and all the good people who surround us. My mom gave me a strong background in my Catholic faith and taught me that if we believe, everything will work out.

Every day is a blessing given to us by God. I'm grateful that the God Bumps I experienced along the way reinforced those beliefs and will forever give me peace.

Jay Leintz

Chapter 4

A Voice

*"And you will seek for Me and find Me,
when you search for Me with all your heart,"
Jeremiah 29:13. When I think of that verse,
I am reminded of the two major events
that were God Bumps in my life.*

Afghanistan 2006: We were preparing for what we had been training for all our military careers. Our mission started off with a Fragmentary Order - the Afghan National Army was to carry the trailer with supplies for our three-week mission to the border of Afghanistan. Suddenly, everything changed, and now we would be hauling the supplies instead. At that moment, I heard a voice say, "You are the target," yet, strangely enough, I was overwhelmed with a feeling of warmth and comfort. I made a quick call to my son to wish him a happy birthday and tell him I loved him – and we were off.

My crew and I rehearsed Improvised Explosive Device (IED) drills over and over again. We had 28 vehicles plus other assets to protect. My gunner looked to me for guidance as to which direction to ace his weapons system. I heard that voice again, telling me that turning the weapons to the left was the correct answer. I relayed it like an order from my commander. Ten minutes out of the gate, and the voice assured me that everyone would be protected. I was concerned about the amount of traffic and the number of civilians in the vicinity, but I did not feel fearful. I pushed Record on my camera as we approached the bridge.

We passed the first vehicle with no problems, but when we passed the second vehicle, a loud explosion rang out. It was strong enough to lift the Humvee off its wheels, pull open the doors and break the combat locks. Fire danced around us for what seemed like a long time, but the seat belts held, and all inside were safe.

My gunner took a minor amount of shrapnel to his cheek from his nose to his chin. He was going to have a scar, but had he been facing the other direction with less armor I know he would not be with us today. In all, nine civilians lost their lives, including the suicide bomber in the vehicle. The Explosive Ordinance Disposal crew would later tell us what saved us. Apparently, the bomber placed 500 lbs. of mortar rounds right side up instead of side to side. This caused the blast to go up and over, rather than directing the blast directly into us.

I prayed for all who died that morning, including for the soul of the man who wanted to take our lives. I am profoundly grateful for hearing God's voice that day. It has brought me much healing over the years. and I listen every day for Him to speak to me.

Iraq 2009: I was close to going home on leave and so

ready to spend a few weeks with my family. It was supposed to be just another day; pick up the trucks, roll out the gate, and head home. Our convoys averaged 100 trucks but only had seven gun trucks, so we had our work cut out for us.

It had been awhile since I had the feeling of warmth and comfort that I have when God whispers in my ear. Today I heard it, warning me that I should take the gun. I looked at my gunner, who is nearly 6 ft. 7 in. The turret shield offered him little protection.

I suggested to my convoy commander that we give these future leaders a chance to lead, as we were nearing the end of our deployment. He liked that idea and took the gun as well. We headed out, and I heard the voice say, "You all will be safe."

In an area not typical for IEDs, we got hit – this time with an Explosive Formed Projectile on a garage door sensor. The first gun truck opened the circuit, and our vehicle closed the circuit. It was a 20 lb. formed projectile, but it had the force of a car crash at 65 mph. The projectile somehow went off before the front wheels closed the circuit, and it hit about 20 feet in front of us.

My shoulder was torn, my ribs were separated, and my heart felt like Mike Tyson punched it. But other than that, we all walked away alive. When we went back to look, there was a perfect halo of shrapnel around where my head was, but not one piece struck me or my helmet. Later when I was at home, I looked in the mirror.

The bruises on my face were shaped like two perfect handprints - as if an unseen force had grabbed me and pulled me down at exactly the right moment. Now that's a God Bump, for sure!

Every morning I wake up to the beauty of a new day. As God's perfect sun rises, I say a prayer of love and gratitude for all He has done for me and my family. I hear people complain daily about every little thing instead of being grateful for what they have. I see children who have so much, and I am reminded of the children in other parts of the world who have nothing. Yet they never ask for more than a high five.

I am convinced we can all experience some God Bumps along the way if we just listen carefully for His Voice. Once you have heard it, you will come away with more compassion for others and a greater appreciation for enjoying life. My advice: Get up early tomorrow and watch the sunrise. You never know what you might see – or hear!

Kevin Niemann

Chapter 5

Jacob's Ladder

"He looked at me as if to say,
'I'll take care of your baby for
you because I truly love him.'"

I was 24 years old when our first child – a boy – was born prematurely. He weighed 3 lbs. 4 oz. My father-in-law was a M.D. and delivered the baby, and he immediately baptized him. Baby Al's weight went down to 2 lbs. 15 oz. but then started its climb to five pounds, at which time he was able to come home with us.

It was a wonderful day, but the start of a grueling regimen that required feeding the baby every hour and a half. My husband, Al, was a dentist and needed his sleep, so it was up to me to do most of the feedings.

During my pregnancy, I mentioned to a friend that I needed to establish a nickname for Al III so no one would call him some ridiculous name like Alley Cat. Being very resourceful, she suggested we call him Tripp (for triple). It was perfect, and it became our tiny baby's nickname.

Tripp was a happy baby. He seldom fussed and put on weight at a good pace. We were relieved that he was doing well and seemed to have none of the problems that can make a "preemie's" growth problematic.

One morning when Tripp was seven weeks old, I finished a feeding and laid him down in the nursery. I went about my day as usual and started to make our bed. I was extremely tired, and the bed looked very inviting. I decided to lie down for just a few minutes. I don't know how long I slept, but when I finally awakened, it occurred to me that it must be time for a feeding. When I went to the nursery and picked up the baby, I noticed that his color didn't look right. He wasn't responding to me, and I knew something was terribly wrong.

In a state of horror, I called my sister-in-law, who lived a few blocks away. She called a doctor whose office was near and they both came right over. You can imagine that I was in a state of shock when the doctor told us that our precious Tripp was dead. I just couldn't believe it! How could this happen?

The next few days are a blur. I held myself together as best I could, except for the burial where I crumbled momentarily. When we got home, we discovered that my in-laws had transformed the nursery back into an ordinary guest room. There was no trace of the sweet baby who inhabited it for the nearly two months of his short life. My in-laws were kind people, but the suggestion was obvious. Life should return to normal, which did not now include that precious little being.

They later determined it was Sudden Infant Death Syndrome that took our baby away from us. We knew little about SIDS because it was a new theory at the time, which added to the pain. Then came the soul-searching because I had fallen asleep. Could I have saved our precious Tripp if I hadn't been sleeping when he needed me? Would I have heard something? If he had been sleeping on his back, would he have been ok? For years, mothers had placed babies on their stomachs to sleep so that they wouldn't inhale foreign matter if they spit up. Now that has become a "no-no." The guilt was agonizing.

I had been a very private person in my relationships with others, so I now put up a façade that we had returned to life as usual. But I must not have done a good job of hiding my feelings because my father-in-law asked me if I blamed myself for Tripp's death. I lied. I told him that I didn't and that everything was fine. My grief was my private world that I shared with no one. My husband was grieving, too, and I didn't want to make his life any more complicated by burdening him with my anguish.

We resumed our regular routine over the next few months. We painted the trim on the house, and I did a lot of sewing. I could immerse myself in sewing because I had bought some very pretty, expensive material. I had to concentrate on what I was doing so I wouldn't ruin it.

Summer was just around the corner, so to take our minds off our loss, we spent lots of time on the

Shrewsbury River. We enjoyed fishing, waterskiing and often just cruising on the river. It's a lovely part of New Jersey, not far from the ocean, with many beautiful summer homes.

The day I'll never forget was gorgeous. There was just a little breeze; it was sunny with a lazy kind of warmth. The day would have been perfect, but I kept having the feeling that a big part of my life was missing. I was immersed in my private grief, longing for that special baby who, by now, would have been crawling, playing and laughing with us.

Al decided he'd like to go on a leisurely cruise down the river and back, so I settled down to do some cloud-watching. As the afternoon wore on, some beautiful, billowy clouds floated across the sky, and I thoroughly enjoyed watching them. My attention was drawn to a wonderful Jacob's Ladder that seemed to be forming. In the Bible, Jacob had a dream about a ladder that rested on earth and reached to heaven. I clearly saw that ladder taking shape in the clouds, taking up most of the eastern sky.

As I watched it take form, I suddenly saw something moving in the center of the ladder. Then, to my amazement, I saw Jesus walking through the ladder with Baby Tripp in His arms. He looked at me as if to say, "I'll take care of your baby for you because I truly love him."

I think God Bumps are little instances when He gets our attention with some special happening that reminds us that He loves us and watches over us. I didn't tell anyone about this special day for years because I believed people would think I was just a distraught mother who had imagined it all. But once I did start telling people about my miracle, I was amazed at their response. They were genuinely excited to hear about it and encouraged me to share it with others.

If you've lost a baby or a child, I believe Jesus wants me to tell you about my God Bump so that you know He cares and is watching over your precious little one. I sincerely hope sharing my story helps bring you peace, as experiencing it did for me.

Jenece Reiman

Chapter 6

The Best is Yet to Come

*"In that instant, it felt like everything
that had been bothering me
was lifted and carried away."*

A long, long time ago in the great state of North Dakota,
a baby was born in a stable. Oops, wrong story! In 1956,
I was born in a Williston, ND, hospital to wonderful,
young parents. They named me David and dedicated
themselves to loving and caring for me. It was if they
had heard God say, "This baby will grow into a man that
you will be pleased with, though he may get into trouble
from time to time. Keep loving him and forgiving him as
I have done."

In 1973 during my senior year of high school, I accepted
Christ at a Southern Baptist Church with two of my
best friends. It is an awesome experience when the Holy
Spirit comes into your life. My life forever changed that
day, but as often happens I started to backslide.

At 19 I married Sandi and that changed things again
for the better as Sandi was a blessing in my life. We had
our first child when I was 21. A baby added joy and
responsibility, and soon two more children entered our
household. We functioned as a normal family, attending
church, school, sports, etc. I was a Sunday school

teacher for 15 years, a coach and a referee, all while working and raising three kids with my wife, who was running a daycare out of our home.

But life changed abruptly when Sandi's dad was diagnosed with cancer and died. Two years later my dad died as well. He was my best friend, and my life went into a tailspin. I tried hard to be strong for my family, especially my mom, but these events took their toll on me. I had lost the two people I had admired and looked up to most, and I was worried that I would be next.

My thoughts and emotions started to change within me, and I began to doubt myself, my wife, my children, my mom and even God. I prayed all the time to change my outlook and attitude. "God, where are you?" I pleaded, "Why can't you help me?" I went into a deep depression: I couldn't sleep; I couldn't eat. I was still trying to function as a husband, father and son while going to work every day. I lost 30 pounds in a month, and everyone was worried about me.

God was there all the time, but I didn't realize it. One morning around Christmas, I was so depressed, that I was on my hands and knees in the bathroom, crying and sobbing. I stood up and looked at myself in the mirror and suddenly saw Christ's face. I heard Him say, "Dave, I have seen your pain, and I want to help. Your dad is with me, and it is time for you to start following me again." Then the image of Dad appeared, and he told me he was with our Father in Heaven, and I must get over my thoughts of dying and start living again.

In that instant, it felt like everything that had been bothering me was lifted and carried away. It was the best feeling I have ever had. I thanked Jesus for rescuing me. It seemed clear that it had been Satan putting these thoughts of dying into me. "No more, Satan," I said, "you have no place in my life. Through Jesus Christ I command you to leave." Just like that, I was healed. I started over, a new being, with a new purpose to follow Jesus the rest of my life. I committed to Him: to obey Him, to listen to Him and to tell others about Him.

But I was to have more challenges in my life: Our daughter, Kaija, was diagnosed with Type 1 Diabetes at the age of seven. At 25, she was diagnosed with progressive MS and is now confined to a wheelchair.

In 2009, I lost my business partner to a heart attack. He was 59 years old, and we had just spent two weeks on a business trip in Europe.

In 2010, my mother was diagnosed with ALS, and she has since passed into the arms of Jesus.

In 2011, my oldest son, Justin committed suicide. He left behind the love of his life, Jodee, and his young son, Vaughn, a toddler at the time.

In January 2012, Sandi was diagnosed with pancreatic cancer and entered heaven on July 22nd of that year. In August of 2019, my life turned upside down again. I remember not feeling well in early August. Yet I drove to Minneapolis to attend a Vikings preseason game with my grandson. I stayed at my sister's place, and I broke out in a sweat and was running a temperature of 102. Being the stubborn Norwegian I am, I was still determined to go to the football game. I remember climbing the stairs to our seats and having to stop every six stairs to make it. We were three rows from the top, which is a long way up at 1st Bank Stadium.

I got through the game and went back to my sister's house. The next morning, I was feeling worse and still feverish, but I drove back to Bismarck anyway. I just wanted to get home and go to bed. I told myself that if I didn't feel better after a good night's sleep, I would go to the doctor.

I made it home and went to bed on August 20th, and that's the last thing I remember for 22 days. On September 4th, I opened my eyes and saw my son Tanner looking at me. I asked, "Why are you here, and where the heck am I?" He explained that I had been in an induced coma for the past three weeks while doctors tried to determine what was wrong with me and how to treat it.

Apparently, my brother took me to the walk-in clinic on August 20th, and they sent me to the emergency room right away, as I was running a 104 temperature. I was hospitalized, and Tanner explained that I was so sick that he was told to call the family because the doctors weren't sure if I was going to pull through. I was having a hard time believing all this, but Tanner asked me what day it was, and I didn't know. He gave me my phone, and

I couldn't remember my passwords. It was obvious that I had a long journey to recovery.

While I was in the coma, doctors determined I had Legionnaire's Disease, which is a high-grade pneumonia. It is transmitted when you breathe in water molecules containing an extremely aggressive bacteria that attaches to your lungs. In most cases, it comes from hotels and cruise ships transmitted through their air-conditioning systems.

The North Dakota Health Department contacted me after I was out of ICU to find out where I might have been exposed to the bacteria. I was not in a hotel or on a cruise ship within the last three months, so we ruled that out. I do not have central air conditioning in my home, so we ruled that out. I thought maybe the YMCA because it could be transmitted through a hot tub or sauna. But we ruled that out since nobody came down with it during that period. In fact, the Health Department officer mentioned that they have had only one other person diagnosed with Legionnaire's disease within the last three years. So where did I pick up the bacteria? Eventually, we determined it came from my Koi pond in my back yard. I remembered cleaning it about two weeks before I got sick.

As I reflected on all that happened and visited with my family and friends, I learned that hundreds of people had been praying for me at the hospital and all over the world. I am living proof that prayers work. Our Father had me in his hands, watching over me and guiding the doctors and nurses. I am so grateful.

I had no idea what a challenge rehab would be. I had to learn to walk again, hold a pen, and try to remember things. I spent one week in the hospital doing rehab and another week in a nursing care facility. I staring to get depressed as I was in rehab with many people recovering from strokes as well as many residents with dementia and Alzheimer's. I witnessed great need and saw people who lacked the ability to do most things.

I knew I would recover, but that many of them may not. I prayed for them and for myself. I worked hard to get my strength back: riding a stationary bike, lifting weights and walking, walking and more walking. All the time my faith continued to grow, even though I was already a spiritual, faithful, and obedient servant to Jesus. During my walks outside, I had many conversations with our Father. I thanked him for sparing me, helping me in the recovery process and asked him why he kept me alive. I was inspired and curious about what the next steps would be to grow with him. Little did I know, when I returned home, I would find out why he had spared me. God had a plan for that that would change my life.

After I was discharged from the nursing care facility, I continued rehab at home. I started receiving many calls from people checking in to see how I am doing. This became a daily routine of sometimes 20 to 30 calls per day. I didn't know I had that many friends! I tried to be respectful and answer as many calls as I could or try to call them back within the next day.

One day I received a call from Jeff, a business associate and friend from Minnesota. Like most of the conversations, it started out with "how are you doing?" My reply to everyone was happy to be here talking to you. When Jeff asked me that question, I picked up something different in his voice. He sounded down, and as we talked more, he opened up to me.

Jeff told me that he was very depressed because of an issue that had been going on for more than two years with a federal government agency that owed him $3 million. He lost his business, was at the point of losing his home, and his wife was ready to leave him. He said, "Dave, it's over; I can't live this way anymore. I have not slept for more than two hours over the course of a couple of months. So, I need to end it. "

I was alarmed and told Jeff that it was not his decision to make. I said God will determine when it's your time to leave this earth, not you. He asked me what he should do. I prayed for the right words to come to me. I implored him to seek medical help immediately. He said he didn't like doctors. I said, "God put doctors on earth to help others, and you need help NOW." I told him I thought doctors would likely be able to give him medication that would help. I advised him that he needed to get connected with a support group or church. He said he was a Christian but hadn't been to church for years. My heart leapt when I heard what he said next. "For you, Dave I will do both: contact my doctor and my church, and I will do it after this call."

I waited anxiously for Jeff to call me back. I heard from him a day later, and it was a great call. I could hear in his voice that he was back to the Jeff I knew. I asked him what happened. He told me that he called his doctor right after our call and got in to see him that day. He said that was a miracle because usually it takes a couple of weeks to get an appointment.

Jeff's doctor confirmed that he was depressed, assured him it was treatable and prescribed medication right away. He said he slept all night, woke up refreshed with no worries and lots of energy. Jeff said it was a miracle: he felt great and had a positive attitude. He said he talked with the church and will be attending again, and he was getting involved with a men's group: another miracle.

I told Jeff I was proud of him and glad he took my advice. He said, "Dave, you saved my life that day we talked, because if you had not answered my call, I would not be talking with you today." I said it was God who saved his life, I was just a messenger. He then said, "I know why God kept you alive, it was for me." That brought me to my knees, and when I thought about it, I realized what Jeff said was right on.

What an awesome Father we serve! God knew that healing me meant I could be there for Jeff. I thank him every day for keeping me alive, although I would have been fine if he had decided to bring me home. But if he had, I would not have been able to say goodbye or see you later to my family. I would not have been able to answer Jeff's call and offer some advice. Who knows what God has in store for me and for any of us? So, live every day as if it will be your last. Thank him for this day and always listen for his voice, which may come in many forms and from many people.

If I could boil down all that I've learned in my life to one formula, I would call it the Four Fs: Our Father in Heaven, Faith, Family and Friends. At times we may feel that God is not part of our lives, but that is because we have not allowed Him into them. He loved us before we were born and will continue to love us on this earth and beyond. He is planning something big for us in Heaven, and I can't wait for the party. The best is yet to come.

God put that message on my heart during one amazing moment, the God Bump that has defined and sustained me every day since then. I miss my family members and friends, who have gone to Heaven, but I was blessed to have them in my life, and I know I will see them again. God bless everyone who reads this. You are a gift to the world and a child of God. Remember that He is with us, through the good times and bad times, through the joy and the hardships. And when it's our turn to walk through those pearly gates, He will be there with open arms. Indeed, the best is yet to come.

Rockin' Dave, Rockin' Back and Rockin' On

Dave Blair

Chapter 7

When Heaven Calls, You Listen

"Then I suddenly realized there was much more to it than that. It was the sign I had asked God to send!"

Brittany was such a beautiful baby with those big, brown eyes and little button nose. She was a funny little girl who brought so much life to our family. Then things changed, and we went through some very turbulent teen years. My husband Gene and I were often at our wit's end.

At age 16, Brittany got pregnant and had Gavin. It was hard to accept at first, but he turned out to be the best thing that ever happened to her and to us. Gavin was a happy, healthy, fun little boy. When he was six, Brittany and Gavin moved to the oil field country of North Dakota. We thought she was stable, and although life was hard, she seemed to be doing well.

Then one Sunday evening two years later, we got the call that changed our lives forever. Brittany had taken her own life. A whirlwind of events followed, including becoming Gavin's guardian. Grieving and adjusting to our new lives took time.

I did a lot of soul searching and digging into the Bible that winter. I needed to know exactly where my baby girl was. Purgatory? Somewhere else? Heaven? I prayed and asked God to reveal to me very clearly what the answer was. I really needed to know!

It took months before I had the heart to disconnect her cell phone service. It was so hard because it seemed to be my only connection left to her. Then one day about two weeks later, Gavin took my phone and said, "Siri, text my mom Brittany." Her number was still in my phone, so Siri brought it up. I almost stopped him, but thought, oh well, it's disconnected. It won't go anywhere.

 He texted her in his precious way, "From Gavin. I love you." A few seconds later, my phone went "Bing!" I couldn't believe it. I grabbed the phone and was shocked when I read the text. It said, "What? Who is this? This is Heaven." You could have knocked me over with a feather!

After typing a few texts with trembling fingers, we discovered that Heaven was the girl's name on the other end of the phone. She must have gotten Brittany's number. Then I suddenly realized there was much more to it than that. It was the sign I had asked God to send!

I texted back and explained that we had lost our daughter six months ago, and her little boy had sent the text. We ended up Facetiming for at least 20 minutes with a beautiful, blonde 12-year-old girl named Heaven Leigh. She sat on her bed with her friend as she chatted with us. And guess what her friend's name was? Destiny! We had a great conversation.

I had several other experiences before that as I anguished over my daughter, but nothing concrete. After this experience, I really felt that I knew where my Brittany was. God knew this mama needed a sign, and He answered my heart's deepest prayers. God Bump! After all, it's not every day that your number goes straight to Heaven – and Heaven answers!

Shar Dukart

Chapter 8

Cool Breeze Brings God Bumps

"I'm a believer; it had to be a divine expereince; there is no other explanation."

It was nearly 100 degrees on that late July day in 1993. I was working as a telephone employee, inspecting fiberoptic cable plow trains. My job was to go ahead of the plow train on the cable easement with a locator stick and mark the existing cable. I had just ducked under a tree, and suddenly, I felt a cold blast of air hit me. It stopped me in my tracks.

I turned around to see what it could possibly be and was shocked to see my dad standing there. I couldn't believe my eyes because my dad had passed away in October 1987. But there he was, dressed in his familiar work clothes, no tie, and wearing his glasses. The shape of his body was clear, and his color was natural, but I could see through him.

He was standing very close to me and gave me a big smile. He didn't speak, but somehow I got a message, "Everything is going to be okay." I shook my head and blinked, and as suddenly as he had appeared, he was gone. As soon as he disappeared, it got warm again.

I didn't know what to think. I started to cry, trying to understand what had just happened. I had so many questions. Why did he come back? Why that message? What was going to be okay? My life? My family?

I didn't question seeing him though. It was real; I wasn't hallucinating. My father came to me in a vision, and I loved seeing him. I've tried to tell others about it, but they have a hard time believing it. However, every time I talk about it, the same chill comes over me. I'm right back there, reliving that amazing experience once again.

I am still confused as to why Dad came to me in this way, but I'm happy he did. I feel blessed to have had the life I've had, and especially that I had this God Bump moment. I'm a believer; it had to be a divine experience; there is no other explanation. To me, that's what God Bumps are all about: something so out of the ordinary that you have to see it, to feel it, to believe it. It just proves to me that even when we don't understand all that life throws our way, if we just have faith, everything will indeed be okay.

Don Boehm

Chapter 9

In God's Time

*"It's funny how we try to do God's work for Him.
It wasn't good enough for me to be
on God's timing. I wanted my own timing,
and it didn't work out so well."*

One would think there would be a definitive definition
for a God Bump. When life throws stones at you, day
after day, year after year, and you come through all of
the brokenness and look back and say, "Only by the
Grace of God am I alive today." Then you know there
are a lot of God Bump moments along the way, so one
definition does not do it justice.

My husband and I were married in 1999. Shortly
afterwards, I found out that we probably could not have
children. When I was 11, I was hospitalized for three
months, while I had surgeries and took medication
for life-threatening conditions. I took correspondence
studies, so I could I make it through 4th grade and not
be left behind the rest of my classmates. As a teenager, I
was diagnosed with PCOS-Polycystic ovary syndrome. It
is a hormone disorder that can affect a woman's ability
to have babies. It can cause periods to be anything from
non-existent to severe and increase one's chances for
other serious health problems. I was put on a birth
control pill for 15 years, which helped regulate bleeding.

However, I was eventually diagnosed with insulin resistance, which led to a diabetes diagnosis.

Not having children was a sad thought when just starting married life, and as the years went by, it became more devastating. I don't think it seemed real right away because we were young. I came from a broken home and was the oldest child. I took care of my siblings, and I have to admit that I sometimes wondered if I really wanted children of my own. I went back and forth on the matter in my mind. My husband had a more stable family life, but we just were not sure at the beginning of our lives together.

Two years into our marriage, we decided to try and get pregnant, but it didn't happen. I went to a fertility doctor for two months and had a procedure to see if pregnancy was a possibility for me. It turned out that it certainly was still in the cards! Unfortunately, the ovulation medication they prescribed made me a little crazy, and it did not seem worth the pain.

It's funny how we try to do God's work for Him. It wasn't good enough for me to be on God's timing. I wanted my own timing, and it didn't work out so well. We decided that if it was meant to be for us, then it would happen. If we weren't to have children, the decision wasn't going to be up to us. I had no real church connection at the time, but I knew from growing up in church life, it was up to God and out of our hands.

We went on with our careers. Along the way, we both had many medical issues: chronic illnesses, surgeries and so much more. In 2010 I developed uterine fibroids that were as big as softballs. Birth control was not keeping them at bay anymore. A gynecologic surgeon wanted to schedule a hysterectomy right away. I said I'd call her with a date in mind, but God had other plans.

On Thanksgiving Day 2010, I woke up in the middle of the night with stabbing pain in my gut. I shot out of bed like a prairie dog out of its hole. I made it through the night, but I worried about all the things that could be wrong. I decided the first thing I should do in the morning was to take a pregnancy test, just in case. I had a stash in the cupboard because being "late" with PCOS was a common thing. We were always hopeful, but I had taken at least 100 tests over the years. I decided, well, we will probably be let down for the 101st time, but I needed to do it.

The time ticked by, and when it was up, I looked at the test, and for the first time, it was positive! There was a little "plus sign" on the stick! I did it again, and it was positive again. I honestly thought it was not real. But God was clearly saying, "Neener, neener, it's time for a baby!" God Bump!

My husband was in the shower, as we were about to go out for Thanksgiving dinner. I knocked on the door and told him I had some news. "We're going to have a baby!" We looked at the test in disbelief. I thought how profound it was: The day we give thanks is the day we found out we were going to have a baby. We truly had something to celebrate and be grateful for this year.

I was in awe, and I was scared. I really thought because of all my medical issues, I was a broken human being. I knew I wasn't in control, and that God was. But I had questions. I felt like I didn't know anything anymore.

My family practice doctor knew my history, and we were friends. I told her I had a positive test, and she actually didn't believe me right away! She sent me to the clinic for a blood test, and it indeed came back positive as well! She told me that it would be a high-risk pregnancy, and that it may be ectopic. This is when the fertilized egg grows in an area outside the uterus, and it's very dangerous for the mother. Based on some of the symptoms that I was having at the time of the blood draw, she said that could be the case. The doctor then gently said she could give me a shot to end the pregnancy.

I was devastated! How could this be happening? I wanted to keep this little peanut growing as long as possible until we knew for sure that it was a life-threatening pregnancy. As far as I was concerned, it was just another event in a long string of medical events where God could have taken me home. I cried a lot, but decided I was going to take my chances because it may be the only chance I get.

We got through the weekend and went back to the doctor on Monday morning after a few stressful days of "what if" scenarios dancing through our heads. But the blood work turned out great, and the ectopic pregnancy threat was gone. The doctors had been nervous about it because the hormone numbers weren't doubling like they should have been. In the end, the obstetrician decided that it was because there likely were twins, which can keep numbers from doing their thing from the beginning. Oh, how wonderful it would been to have two babies at once, but this pregnancy was high risk even for one. Again, God had a plan, and the doctors believed that sometime during the weekend, one of the twins did not survive. By the time we went to the doctor on Monday, the numbers had returned to normal.

Kara was born in July of 2011, shortly after my 36th birthday. My husband and I look back at how blessed we were, and we know we were not in control at all. Scripture tells us to not be anxious! This is so true! Let God do the work. Try to listen. It can be so hard! Everything is in God's time. God Bumps!

Angie Milakovic

Chapter 10

In Loving Memory of Paige

*"I pray that my pain does not go to waste.
I hope that through it I can be stronger
and more open to do God's will."*

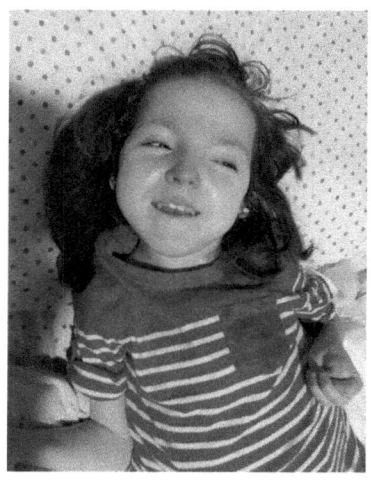

Seeing your child for the first time defines complete and pure love. Losing that child defines complete and pure sorrow. The loss makes you want to beg for physical pain instead of the pain that comes from within the soul.

God Bumps to me are when we fully understand how little influence we have over our lives and how much we need Him to navigate through the roughest times. I never would have thought my family and I could hurt so badly, but I pray that my pain does not go to waste. I hope that through it I can be stronger and more open to do God's will. My daughter would not want me to be in such sorrow the rest of my life.

Paige was born with some health issues. But after an operation at 10 months, she had an unnatural hypoxic event, meaning her brain was deprived of oxygen, causing brain damage. It was difficult for us to accept and to forgive those who allowed this to happen. However, we knew that, without forgiveness, we would not be able to fully care for her. She made me a better person and more compassionate. I have come to believe this was God's way of telling us that Paige would complete us and others in a way no one else could. She brought many God Bumps into our lives.

We are a blended family of six, including my wife, Mary, Paige's two younger sisters and an older brother. Before this happened, our lives were a busy fiasco. Suddenly everything came to a halt, and family was all that

mattered. We knew we needed to spend quality time with one another. Paige brought our family together in a way that never would have happened otherwise. She had a way of looking at you, like she was looking into your soul. When I came into the room, her eyes would lock onto mine. In those moments, we completely understood one another. She did not have to call me Dad or tell me that she loved me. I could tell by looking at her beautiful, brown eyes.

We all found ways to cope, and running became my therapy. This made me physically and spiritually stronger to take care of Paige. I ran marathons inspired by her strength. I completed 100-mile races with her waiting for me at the finish line. The suffering I did on the trails pales in comparison to her daily sufferings. I took her everywhere I went and brought her to countless appointments, hoping we could find something that would improve her quality of life. Even a few percentage points of improvement would be well worth it. Together we advocated for medicinal cannabis because of the positive effects for those with epilepsy. I believe her love softened many hearts, and North Dakota did pass the necessary bill.

We experienced several God Bumps when Paige was with us, but when she left us, they were all around us. On Monday night August 14, 2017, we took Paige to high-school orientation, but Mary and I just were not engaged with the task at hand. I cannot explain it except for our underlying intuition – we were both feeling that she would never go to high school.

That night we noticed some swelling in her legs. She had an appointment with her doctor the next day, and they found she had low blood pressure and a urinary tract infection. She was admitted to the pediatric intensive care unit. I slept there overnight and by the morning, they had trouble with IV access. She had sepsis and needed her antibiotics, so they did a picc (percutaneous indwelling central catheter) line with me by her side. She was later intubated secondary to the sedation.

Her condition worsened, and we made plans to have her flown to the University of Minnesota Hospital. The nurse told me to go home and pack, but I told her I did not need anything but Paige. Within 40 minutes, Paige's blood pressure dropped. I could not feel a pulse and started compressions. The nurse took over for me, and the medical team did everything they could to bring her back. Mary and I were there beside her. After two minutes of compressions and no shockable rhythm, I looked at Mary, and she nodded. She told Paige that if it was too hard, she should go. Paige went to Heaven at that very moment.

I do not think Paige wanted to get on that plane, and as hard as it was, I am thankful to have been there with her and Mary. But it also was pure agony because I couldn't help but feel that Paige would be better off with me. Early in the morning on the day after Paige died, I could not sleep. Sorrow upon sorrow washed over me, and I decided to text my colleagues about the horrible news. Later my colleague Leslie shared that she had a dream the night Paige died, and when she got my text, she burst into tears. "I don't know how to describe the dream – I wasn't in it, but I was watching it unfold," she said. "It was full of light, happiness, and innocence. Every time I fell back asleep that night, I had the exact same dream – it was of a girl wearing a wispy, white, flowered dress – arms out wide, feeling the tall grass and wildflowers running through her fingers. The breeze was blowing her hair and dress gently. She was smiling and giggling. I knew it was Paige because of her big, brown eyes."

This was an amazing God Bump! Paige knew we needed reassurance and interceded through a person who certainly cares but did not know Paige had passed away. The meaning and timing of the dream had to be profound to help me with my deep grief. As a result, I now feel that she is in the best arms imaginable. Everything that was impossible for her on earth is possible now. She is in Paradise without epilepsy, wheelchairs and pain, patiently waiting for us to be reunited. I see her in every sunrise and sunset, and I never feel that she is far away.

On August 16, 2017, Paige went to Heaven. This was a week after my 40th birthday, and I cringed at the contrasting milestones. The news anchors were talking about it being the 40th anniversary of Elvis Presley's death. I cringed again. We were planning her funeral, and I was searching for something significant to mark this date. I asked the church for the video they had taken of Paige's Baptism, even though I really was looking for the video of her Communion. They did not have the video but were amazed to learn her date of Baptism was Aug 16! Wow, I needed that just then to lift me out of the abyss of sorrow. Fourteen years after Paige became a Child of God, she returned home to her Heavenly Father. God Bump!

August 23, 2017, 1:20 PM: My mom always stops at a particular gas station on the way home to South Dakota, and this time was no different. Even though she had plenty of beverages with her, she still stopped in to buy a soda and a brat. She looked at the Diet Coke she had picked out and could not believe what she saw. She started to cry when she saw it had the name Paige on it. This happened on Paige's eighth day in Heaven - to give me comfort that she was more than okay. God Bump!

August 6, 2017: My childhood friend Andy was in town celebrating my 40th birthday 10 days before Paige passed. I had not seen him in years, and we went for a walk along the river. I also had not caught a Monarch caterpillar in years. I had given Paige a balloon with a Monarch butterfly on it on the day she was born. She loved the bright colors. I still have the balloon.
 As Andy and I were walking, we noticed a caterpillar

on some milkweed. Andy picked it up and held it in his hands all the way home where we put it in a jar. That night the caterpillar ate a lot of food. The next day it was in a chrysalis!

On the day of Paige's funeral, going home without her was hard. I sat at the table, feeling empty inside. Something made me look over at the caterpillar's jar. It was almost as if someone had tapped me on the shoulder. I believe it was Paige trying to get my attention. I turned around and saw this beautiful Monarch hanging underneath the lid. It must have just come out because it was not yet able to fly, and the wings had not been battered by the jar. Paige had sent me a sign!

My sister Jennifer was there and looked up how to release it to the wild. We had to wait until the wings were dry. It was a very windy day as it is often is North Dakota. It took a while, but that Monarch took flight, and my sister took a video of it. It was so beautiful! I believe Paige knew I would be worried about her and sent the butterfly to tell me she was more than okay! Death for Paige was not the end but a new beginning. God Bump!

A few days after Paige went to Heaven, I got this message from my friend Scott: "Tracy, I wanted you to know we were praying for you and your family. I went to bed last night and asked God to give you a sign He had your girl, and she was okay. When I woke up, I got a text from my daughter with the same Bible verse that was included in Paige's funeral service. 'I'm convinced that neither death nor life, nor Angels nor Demons, neither the present nor the future nor any powers, neither height nor depth, nor anything else in all creation will be able to separate us from the love of God that is in Christ Jesus our Lord.'" God Bump!

November 9, 2017: I usually go for a run during my lunch hour, and on the way back I often stop at the cemetery and spend some time with Paige. On this particular day, I found a dollar in the snow across from the cemetery. It just so happened that I needed a dollar that day for a company contest! It may seem like a small thing, but to me she either provided it or Jesus provided it to show me that Paige was fine. I did not win the contest, but I was able to get the dollar back because of what it symbolized. God Bump!

Without the ability to walk or talk, Paige was able to love and receive love. To us, she was not disabled at all. We took care of her for 15 years, and she took care of our souls and our humanity. Paige suffered here on earth and has now inherited Heaven. Jesus carried His

cross and was redeemed. Paige also carried her cross and filled our world with so much love! Now she is in Paradise waiting for us to join her.

God Bumps remind me of her love and the gentle nudges she still sends me. These are the moments when God embraces us and softly whispers that our love for Paige defeated death. Eventually I believe gratitude will replace the melancholy. As each anniversary of her death passes, it gets a little easier. I will always miss Paige, and I will always love her. I know in my heart that she is in God's loving arms and is safe. I am thankful that God Bumps have given me signs that she is doing way better than OK!

Tracy Vearrier
(father)

Chapter 11

Bumps of Grace

"The chapel seemed to fill with light that went straight to my soul. A feeling of unbelieveable warmth flowed through my whole body, and I have no doubt it was the Holy Spirit. I felt completely overcome with joy, peace and love."

The first time I experienced a God Bump moment was while I was singing at my grandmother's funeral. I was in my 20s, and it was the second funeral of a close relative in the past five months for which I was the soloist.

Grandma and I were kindred spirits, united through music. Grandpa had died young, and she lived across the street from my Catholic grade school. She attended daily mass at the church next to the school and sat behind the students seated in the front rows. Grandma Elizabeth (Lizzie to her friends) had a beautiful, first-soprano voice. I loved to hear her sing, as her voice soared high above everyone else and seemed to float there. It was amazing to think that big voice came out of her small body. She was a stout Hungarian woman, about 4'10" with a round shape and chunky legs. She wore babushkas on her head to church in the winter and mantillas in the summer.

Grandma wasn't a very demonstrative person, but she hugged me fiercely on occasion. She and I both liked hot cereal for breakfast; she served it with heavy cream, plus an extra pat of butter to show her love. We both had broken ankles at the same time when I was in grade school. Neither of us was happy about being on crutches, but we were able to joke about our shared situation.

Grandma had a massive stroke coming out of church on a gloomy Sunday in April. I remember one of the three priests who presided at her funeral said that she died in the best way – right after receiving the Body of Christ. Her funeral was well attended even though it had rained for weeks, and the gravel roads in our area were nearly impassable. Our town was a greasy mudhole. My dad laid planks across the street so that we could get to church without sinking in the mud. My aunts, uncles and large extended family traveled from many states, including my Uncle Louie, who had left the family farm to become a successful business leader in Ohio.

As I was singing in the choir loft, I asked God for strength to be able to sing for my grandma without breaking down. I wanted the music to be a beautiful tribute to her and her love of music. I remember looking at the stained-glass windows and noticing that the sun was starting to come out and casting beautiful streams of light onto the congregation.

As I started to sing "On This Day, O Beautiful Mother," something caught my eye. It was my Uncle Louie. I saw his knees give out, and he sank down onto the pew, looking like he was going to faint. My dad and his wife turned to him. I prayed for God's help. I HAD to finish this song despite what was happening in the church below me. It was Grandma's favorite; I learned it at a young age and often sang it with her. I kept going, but my voice started shaking.

On this day, O Beautiful Mother.
On this day, we give thee our love.
Near thee, Madonna, fondly we hover.
Trusting our gentle care to prove.

Suddenly, I felt a beam of light come through the window and shine on my face. A sensation like goosebumps went through my body, starting at the back of my neck and going down to the arm that was holding my music. I felt a sense of calm go through me, and my voice became stronger and stronger. I finished the song with no problem. I looked down at Uncle Louie, and he was now standing upright and had recovered. I know without a doubt, God helped both of us at that moment.

The second time I experienced God Bumps was when I was attending a Catholic weekend retreat called a Cursillo. The weekend is designed to help practicing Christians renew and strengthen their love of Jesus. It is a way to grow in faith, knowledge, and personal holiness. The goal is to bring Christian values to all and to make those values the pattern for our own lives.

The three-day weekend consists of a series of talks

by clergy and lay people. The major emphasis of the experience is to ask participants to take what they have learned back into the world, on what is known as the "fourth day." I listened to the talks during the weekend, searching for the concepts that resonated, hoping that I would come home feeling refreshed and renewed in my faith.

But it wasn't easy. I was distracted by issues at home for which there seemed no solution. Every time I tried to concentrate on the talks, my mind wandered, and worry set in. The one thing that helped pull my attention back was the theme song of Cursillo: "De Colores." It originated as a Spanish folk song honoring farm life and was adopted by the Cursillo movement. De Colores means "in colors," and for Cursillo participants being "in colors" means being in God's grace.

During one of the quiet prayer times, I went to the beautiful chapel in the retreat center. I was disappointed that I didn't seem to be getting as much out of the experience as those around me. I decided to pray about it, to ask God's help in quieting my mind. But one of the issues at home kept coming up, so I abandoned my focus on the weekend and concentrated on that. I prayed for help in dealing with it. I closed my eyes and opened my heart for guidance.

What happened next was amazing. The chapel seemed to fill with light that went straight to my soul. A feeling of unbelievable warmth flowed through my whole body, and I have no doubt it was the Holy Spirit. I felt completely overcome with joy, peace and love. I looked around to see if anyone else was experiencing what I was, but everyone was concentrating on their own prayers. The experience was solely mine, and I knew that God had given me the grace to face any obstacles ahead of me. I walked out of the chapel, feeling almost as if I was floating on air.

On the last day of the retreat, participants are asked to give a short testimony about what they learned or what they were going to take out into the world. Everyone's words were different; all were beautiful. I was extremely nervous; I had no idea how to share what I had experienced. I considered not sharing at all. When my turn came up, I took a deep breath and simply said, "I cannot find the words to describe what happened to me this weekend. So, let me just put it this way..." At that point, I burst out in song, singing "De Colores":

> De Colores (In colors)
> Let us live in grace since we can.
> Let us quench, let us quench
> The burning thirst of the King who does not die.
> De Colores
> Let us bring to Christ a soul and thousand more.

Applause burst out among the retreat goers, and we all walked out ready to share the good news. The best part is that feeling has never left me. All I do is close my eyes and think about that day, and I once again feel the Holy Spirit within me. It's a smaller, more intimate glow of love, but it's there, always burning in my soul.

The third time I experienced God Bumps was when I had to make the most difficult decision of my life. I got engaged at 17 and married at 18. I thought he was the love of my life, and I committed myself fully, even though I had second thoughts during that engagement year. But so many plans had been made, and I didn't want to disappoint anyone, so I went ahead with the marriage.

It was a rocky road. The details aren't important now, but married life was a challenge. Being a good Catholic girl though, divorce was not an option I felt I could consider. So I prayed fervently and tried to make the best of the situation. We stayed together nearly two decades and had three children. They are the lights of my life, and I tried to create a loving home for them, despite the ups and downs.

On Holy Thursday a few months before our 20th wedding anniversary, an event occurred that was the last straw for me. I did not know how we could go on from there. I went to church that night and took my usual spot in the choir. I held back tears during all the songs, trying to figure out what to do. We had company coming for the weekend, and I needed to get through that first.

As we sat for the Homily, I felt a tingle in the back of my neck. It went down my arm to my fingertips. I thought I might be having a stroke. Then I heard a voice in my head saying, "You can leave this marriage. Everything will be ok. I am with you." I knew it was God speaking to me. I felt instantly calm and the tingling went away. I felt the glow of the Holy Spirit in my heart.

At that point, it was time for the Washing of the Feet in the Holy Thursday liturgy. We were singing one of my favorite songs, "As I Have Done For You." These words stood out to me and ran through my head for the rest of the weekend:

You have heard the voice of God
In the words that I have spoken.
You beheld Heaven's glory
And have seen the face of God.

We separated the next week, and over the course of a difficult year, we went through divorce proceedings. I immediately researched the annulment process because I knew I wanted to continue to be part of my church. I had no plans to remarry, but it was important to me to be in good standing with the Catholic Church.

I had heard all kinds of horror stories about the annulment process: how expensive it was, how long it took, how it made people feel, how it would make my children feel, etc. I didn't know what to expect when I went to the Diocesan office to meet with the annulment advisor. She was a very kind woman, and when she handed me the brochure about annulments, I breathed a sigh of relief. The title on the brochure was "The Ministry of Healing." It seemed quite appropriate for my situation, and as I maneuvered the process, I found it to be true. I felt it was like a counseling process, but from the spiritual perspective.

It took about six months for the annulment process to be completed, and the total cost was $250. Meanwhile, God sent a very special man my way, who has indeed turned out to be the love of my life. He was also a divorced Catholic, and once we started talking about marriage, he started his annulment process. Three-and-a half years after that fateful Holy Thursday, we walked down the aisle in our Catholic Church and joined our hearts and our families in Holy Matrimony. At this writing, we have been happily married for 26 years.

My fourth experience with God Bumps came when I made a career move. I had worked in the energy industry for 20 years, and it was time for a change. On a cold January day, I stepped onto the Mayo Clinic campus in Rochester, MN, for my first day as a staff member. I was excited and scared; this was a big step.

First on the agenda was orientation, including campus tours and history lessons. I've always been an artist as well as a singer in my spare time; I was in awe of what I saw across the campus. There was amazing art everywhere: paintings, pottery, sculptures, fiber art, drawings, blown glassworks, and beautiful landscaping. There were baby grand pianos with signs inviting people to play them. There were also quiet places for prayer and meditation, as well as busy historical or patient education centers.

I wasn't quite sure of the connection to healthcare. I came from a publicly traded company, where the bottom line was everything. At first glance, these extra touches seemed frivolous. Fortunately, my job was in communications, so I quickly learned about the Mayo Clinic difference.

Permeating every decision at Mayo Clinic is its primary value: the needs of the patient come first. I learned that meant the needs of the whole patient: body, mind and spirit. For optimum healing, all these needs are considered. A restorative, hospitable environment is critical to the patient's recovery – nearly as critical as the staff's expertise. I learned that most of these artistic elements were donated by grateful patients.

I had a demanding job working with Mayo Clinic leaders, but it wasn't long before I was able to contribute with my whole spirit to patient needs: singing for patients and getting involved with the arts. I can attest to many moments where I felt the song that I sang for a patient contributed to their healing journey. In my department, we received many testimonials about the hospitable environment and employees who went well beyond their job descriptions.

On one particular day, when I was singing for patients over my lunch break, a gentleman in a wheelchair especially caught my eye. His wife was standing behind him, and they had stopped to listen to the music, both smiling broadly. I was singing "I Could Have Danced All Night," and for some reason, I felt the urge to go over to the couple while I was singing. The man reached out his hand, and I took it, continuing to sing. His wife started moving the wheelchair around, and for the rest of the song, it looked like the three of us were dancing together. People all around had stopped what they were doing to watch us and applauded and cheered when the song was over.

But when the music stopped, the man kept holding tightly to my hand. I wasn't quite sure what to do. I looked at my accompanist, who realized what was going on. She played a single chord, and I knew what song we were going to do next. I kneeled next to the man, and started singing:

> I believe for every drop of rain that falls,
> a flower grows.
> I believe that somewhere in the darkest night,
> a candle glows.
> I believe for everyone who goes astray,
> someone will come to show the way.
> I believe. I believe.

Beams of light radiated through the atrium windows of the multi-level Gonda Building and shone on the patient's face. I looked up and saw people leaning over the railings several stories up, watching the three of us and listening to the music. Many were blotting their eyes with tissues. The presence of the Holy Spirit was palpable.

When I finished singing the song, there were a few seconds of complete silence, and then applause. The man patted my hand and said thank you, as I stood up. His wife, with tears rolling down her cheeks, gave me a huge hug, and then they were off to his next appointment. I looked at my watch, and knew I needed to start walking across campus for my next meeting. My heart was glowing with the Holy Spirit for the rest of the day.

I sang for patients many more times during my years at Mayo Clinic and had some wonderful experiences. I sang for dignitaries and community leaders; I sang for children in cancer treatment; I sang for potential benefactors; and I sang for employee groups. But none were quite as memorable as that one beautiful day. The day when, for a few minutes, the bustling world of Mayo Clinic came to a brief halt as we experienced an amazing God Bump moment of grace, crystallized for all of us through one patient and a song.

Linda Donlin

Chapter 12

Love is Always
the Answer

"During all of this, faith was part of my life, but was not at the forefront. Then one day, everything changed."

Never take anything for granted. Ever. Not your parents. Not your health. Not your children. Because at any time, they can all be gone. My God Bumps story could be seen as one of loss. But I think it's really a story of faith and of love. Because, despite the hard times that life gave me, God has always been there, caring for me.

I am the oldest of four children and had a great deal of responsibility. My parents were always working, and it was up to me to take care of my siblings and get the evening meal prepared. I was in many activities, but my parents were never there. I was the one who got everyone ready and to where they were supposed to go. I distinctly remember Parents Night, when I stood there holding a rose to give to my mom and dad, but they never showed up to support me.

Later, in my senior year of high school, I got pregnant. I went on to graduate high school and I did marry my child's father in July of that year because that's what was expected. Our daughter was born in November. However, the marriage was a disaster as he was abusive from the start: drinking, lying, cheating, and forcing me to have sex. We had three more children together, and despite everything, I stayed with him.

After all that, the ultimate insult happened on Christmas Day 1995. Right after we had celebrated Christmas with our families, the sheriff came to our house and served me divorce papers. My husband tried to keep everything from me, including the kids and our belongings. I did get an apartment and the kids and I sat on lawn chairs and slept on the floor. Eventually, it was over, and for the first time in years, I felt safe.

The girls were almost grown when this happened, and the boys chose to live with me. We were a close family, even though times were tough. My parents developed health issues: Mom got cancer and had surgery, and Dad had congestive heart failure. I was sad when Dad passed away, as we had become best friends. But I was also relieved because he had been in a great deal of pain.

During all this, faith was part of my life, but was not at the forefront. Then one day, everything changed. I had always been healthy and going nonstop. Suddenly at work, I didn't feel well at all and decided to go to the doctor. They ran many tests, and the next day the doctor called me and said I needed to go into the hospital right away. I required two blood transfusions and was diagnosed with Stage 4 cervical cancer. I was 48, and my youngest was a freshman in high school at the time.

The kids were all afraid of losing their mom. Their emotions ranged from anger to shock to devastation. It was hard for me to tell my mother that I had cancer because she had just had cancer surgery herself. She was stunned and scared.

But I knew that God had gotten me through so much in my life. I felt that He would be there for me this time too. I was treated locally at first but then went to the University of Minnesota. I had radiation and chemotherapy for four months to shrink the tumor, and then on November 16, the doctors decided it was time for surgery. I put everything in God's hands.

The surgery was grueling. It lasted more than 10 hours, and the recovery was not smooth. I was allowed to come home for Christmas, but had to turn right around as complications set in. For three weeks, nothing worked right. My son Chris, who had already graduated from high school, never left my side. I have permanent issues, including a colostomy and nephrostomy tube catheters. I am required to have procedures to change out the stents to my kidneys – at first, they were every six months, now they are every three weeks.

Chris was my knight in shining armor through all of this. He took off work and drove me 436 miles each way for my doctor visits each month for two-and-a-half years. He made me ramen noodles when that was all I could keep down. He got me get out of bed for radiation treatments when I really didn't want to. It was a heavy burden for someone his age.

Chris came across as a quiet person until you got to know him. He had a few close friends, and unfortunately, they got into substance abuse. He fought that all through high school, went through treatment and eventually found Teen Challenge. It's a Christian-based organization that works with young people going through life-controlling problems. It encourages them to evangelize while applying Biblical principles to their relationships with people and the community. Chris grew in his faith and responded well to that program; he even became a mentor to others and traveled to other states to give testimony.

Things took a turn for the worse, however, when the girl he was in love with started seeing someone else. Their relationship was off and on, and he was struggling. I convinced him to come home, but he was upset about not being with her. She made promises to see him, but it wouldn't happen. They had big plans for Valentine's Day, and once again she never showed. He was brokenhearted.

On February 16, I got the call that is every parent's worst nightmare. Chris had decided to end his life in the river. I was crushed, beside myself with anguish. I went down to the river to look for him on that bitterly cold morning, but it was hopeless. I was devastated, but after thinking about it, I realized the signs had all been there. He made phone calls he didn't usually make. He called my mom to ask how she was doing and told her he loved her. He went through all his things and gave them away or threw them in the dumpster. Later, laying on his bed, we found seven bibles open to different verses. During his Teen Challenge days, he had mentioned thoughts of suicide in his testimony, but we were not prepared for this.

To top it all off, the authorities couldn't find his body. The water was high that year, and the river was flooding. We knew he had entered the river and the chances of survival were slim, but they had to declare him missing and not dead. I knew in my heart he was gone though. We held a candlelight service under the bridge for family and friends. That was a God Bump moment for me because I felt he was no longer suffering.

The following days were difficult. There were news stories about his disappearance. The reporters referred to him as a "distraught young man." The hardest thing was going to the dentist office to get his records for the police file. I remember pulling up in the parking lot and just sitting in my car in tears. I also attended a Survivors of Suicide meeting. After that, I knew in my heart he was gone. Even though he was still considered missing, there was no doubt in my mind that my son was at peace in the arms of the Lord.

Still, it was difficult to get closure. Finally, more than six years later, I got a call to come down to the police department. Some of his remains had been discovered; they had found a skull and femur bone. There was no jawbone, but there was enough intact that the DNA proved it was Chris.

We held a memorial service at the cemetery and buried his remains on top of my dad's. As his remains were being lowered, one of my friends was taking pictures. Suddenly, there was an extremely bright flash, and I knew it was a sign from Chris. He was telling me that he was all right. One of his favorite sayings was, "Keep on pressing on." That was my God Bump closure moment from Chris: "Keep going, Mom. I'm ok."

People ask me how I've come through all this, and my answer is simple. I would never have been strong enough to survive if God was not in my life. I take one day at a time and live every day to the fullest. My life is full of love, full of blessings, full of God Bumps. I tell my loved ones every day, "I love you. I love you more." After all, love is what God gives to us and what we can give to others. Love is always the answer.

Laurie Mann

Chapter 13

Never Say Never

"God's timing was and always is impeccable!"

My first marriage failed miserably. Years later, my God Bumps moments happened when God made me realize there was more in store for me than I ever dreamed possible. His Plan was much bigger than my fear of letting someone get close to me and my unwillingness to ever get married again.

Like most people intend to do, when I got married the first time, I vowed it would be forever. Little did I know that the moment I said I do, my vows literally turned into something that would seem like a life sentence rather than a marriage. I was miserable for the next year and a half until my divorce was final.

Details aren't necessary, so I'll make a long story short: I had fallen victim to a verbal, mental and physical abuser. No, he wasn't like that before we got married, so I was completely taken by surprise when this behavior began. Unfortunately, the same story is heard far too often by far too many. But I was broken enough to stay in that unhealthy situation until I became pregnant.

After our daughter was born, I became a cougar to my

cub and grew a spine. My first God Bump moment came like a wave of unknown strength in me that triggered my instinct to protect and survive. The only thing I cared about was protecting my child from being raised in a violent environment! I refused to let her grow up thinking abuse was normal or acceptable. I left, and we started our lives over again.

This wasn't the first time I had to start over. But this time was different; I had to do it with a child. I had to do it with nothing but a crib and our clothes. I had no car and no job; it was one of the scariest moments of my life. Sure, being in an abusive situation is scary. However, having a helpless human depending on your every decision to have a fair shot in life was far more terrifying to me than anything I'd ever endured. I was always questioning myself about whether I was making the right decisions. Her well-being depended on my every move. I knew she was my purpose, always and forever, and would be my greatest accomplishment.

Thank God for my Momma! Her love, support and strength helped me through those times. Now my daughter is in her twenties, and she clearly survived every decision I made back then. But while we were in the midst of it, I thank God she was too young to know about my mistakes and that I was learning as she grew.

Years passed, and I had my share of failed dating attempts. I had a few long-term relationships during the 15 years I was raising my daughter, but nothing was serious enough to get me to the point of "I do." My marriage view was badly tainted; I viewed it as a "slow death" rather than the beautiful experience it's supposed to be. I often said it would take an act of God before I'd ever get married again. I've since learned not to put limitations on what God can and will do in my life.

I focused on making something of myself while raising my child. I went to college, worked full time and, in the end, it all worked out. I was a little moody and had a few stumbles along the way, but I got an associate's degree in Advanced Medical Terminology, Anatomy and Physiology and Mastering Medical Coding. It wasn't anything to write to the president about, but I did graduate at the top of my class and that meant something to me. It was an accomplishment about which I could say, "I did it!" and I did it with flying colors.

That education helped me better provide for my child and myself over the next 10 years, as I was able to land a fantastic job at the hospital as a medical coder. But little did I know after giving years of my time and hard work to my department, my days were numbered. I was forced to resign from this position because rules at work had changed, and it became a requirement to become certified to continue as a medical coder at the hospital. This test cost a pretty penny, and it was a timed test. I've never tested well, especially under pressure, and I've struggled with ADHD ever since I can remember. Being able to read a mock doctor's report, thumb through three different books to look up medical codes to find the answer to the questions with a clock ticking away was a disaster in the making for me.

I was used to coding reports using the medical coding books program on the computer. It made finding codes faster and easier. Unfortunately, during the certification exam, we were only allowed to use the actual books and not the computer program. Sadly I failed the first time because the clock ran out before I could finish the test. Determined to retest and pass, I joined a study group of co-workers who had also failed the test the first time. I was scared; my job and the means to provide for my child and myself were on the line.

During this period of long, numbing hours of study, working full time, tending to my child and my daily household duties, my stress level was through the roof. But my faith was strong, and I prayed nonstop, trusting that God would see me through yet another rough spot in my life.

One night I hopped on my social media platform and noticed I had a private message waiting in my inbox. I was surprised and shocked to see it was someone I knew 20 years ago. His message read, "Hey, you remember me?" Of course I remembered him! How we knew each other is a long story, but the fact that he popped up out of the blue, at this time, couldn't have been more perfect. How he found me or why didn't matter to me. God's timing was and always is impeccable! I needed a friend; someone who made me laugh and smile. I needed someone to help take my mind off the stress I was going through. He was all those things.

We had grown up in the South, but I was living in the North at the time. And though distance kept us apart, we grew closer with every conversation we had over the phone. We talked endlessly, trying to catch up on 20 years of lost time. He asked me when I planned to come back to my roots. I told him my intentions were to move home after my daughter finished school. He asked me if he could fly up to visit me, and I said yes. He flew over 2,000 miles to see me and meet my daughter.

Things blossomed between us from there. Because of my first marriage, trust did not come easy for me. But I instantly felt comfortable just being myself around him. When I was a teenager, he was one of my closest friends. So instantly I had a trust in him that was planted when we were kids. He knew who I was from years ago, and though we both had matured over the years, we were the same people. He knew the trials I'd been through, and that I was vulnerable. However, I felt safe around him, which made it easy to fall in love with him.

Time went by, and we decided to try to make the long-distance relationship thing work for us. February 24th was the day we decided to commit to each other. He knew my current situation with my job, and the crucial test for which I was preparing. He was supportive but concerned for mine and my daughters' well-being if I didn't pass this test. I joked that maybe we'd move south if I didn't pass this test. Who knows what the future has in store, I teased.

I wasn't worried though. I had all the confidence in the

world that I was going to pass this test. I felt it was God's Plan. I felt more prepared than I did the first time, and even more prepared than when I took my final exam in college. I whipped through that test with a half-hour left to spare. I couldn't have been happier to be done with that obstacle. Now all I had to do was wait a couple days to find out my results. That was nerve racking, but not as much as the test itself.

Results were in…. my heart sank, and my confidence vanished. I failed by three points. I cried, got angry, and felt sorry for myself. This pity party went on for a couple days, until panic hit me like a ton of bricks. What was I going to do? I snapped back into survival mode after I had my fill of "poor me."

I knew it was time to move on to the next chapter of my life! I wiped my tears, straightened myself up and started planning like I'd always done when I had to start over. I talked it over with my daughter, and we decided to sell the house, pack up and move back to my roots.

Over the next three years, Mr. Blast from the Past, my daughter and I gelled into a happy family. We had some ups and downs, but that was to be expected with a teenager and a drastic change in our lives. Two years after we started dating, he proposed to me and my next God Bump moment happened. A rush of warmth and calm came over me. Eighteen years after my divorce, I said YES to his marriage proposal without a doubt in my heart!

We planned our future ceremony, and in the process, bought a house. Our closing date on our house (oddly enough) was February 24th. It was the same date we started dating. This day became significant to us, so we decided to get married the following February 24th. We have now celebrated six years since our journey began and three years of wedded bliss.

With everything I have been through, the significant changes in my life can only be described as God Bumps: moving from one side of the country to the other, gaining a husband and two more children I love as much as if I'd given birth to them, plus three beautiful grandchildren that I'm completely obsessed with and who call me G'ma. My daughter gained an extra dad who would do anything for her, siblings that have her back no matter what, plus two nephews and one niece.

I may not have passed that coding test, but I did pass the test of trusting in God's Plan. We may think we can choose what we do with our lives, but we really don't have control over God's plans for us. I've learned to "Never Say Never!" If we open our hearts and be aware of the God Bumps along the way, things will eventually work out the way they were meant to be.

Jenna 'Rae Arden

Chapter 14

Restored and Redeemed

*"Although we don't always understand how,
I know without a shadow of a doubt
that Jesus restores us. His word is true,
and He keeps His promises."*

To me, God Bumps are the moments in life when you feel the Lord is so close there is no way to deny His presence. It's the moment you have been asking for, but until now all there seemed to be was silence. Then when that planned, perfect timing of the Lord happens, and He shows up in a tangible way, it is so much greater than anything you could ever have imagined.

I wrestled with what to share because there have been many times in my life when the Lord has restored and redeemed me. It was hard to know which God Bump story He might want me to tell. I wanted to say them all out loud and proclaim the victory Jesus has already given me, in the hope of helping others find restoration and redemption.

Although we don't always understand how, I know without a shadow of a doubt that Jesus restores us. His word is true, and He keeps His promises.
Sexual abuse was a recurring theme in my past. The key

words in that statement are "in the past," because for so long I used to define who I was by what happened to me. It kept me stuck for many years. It was truly crippling to align myself with something so negative. God was calling me to a life of freedom and joy, and I couldn't fully dive into the beautiful gift that He gave me.

I talked about wanting to be free and joyful and not let the abuse rule my life, but I didn't know how. I wanted to say something, but I was afraid that I wouldn't be believed. I feared that what happened to me wasn't a big enough deal to be acknowledged.

The thought of opening up in detail about what happened was repulsing, but the Lord kept pushing, telling me I was worth being truthful and vulnerable. I thought there was no way that I could speak up without completing shattering the bottle inside me where I had sealed all of my emotions. And I was right: opening up about the sexual abuse completely shattered every ounce of okayness that I felt.

But God met me in the midst of the sorrow and grief I felt. Grief from sexual abuse may seem like a weird word to describe what I was feeling. But it definitely was grief, because I didn't realize how truly violated I had been until I talked about it. I realized then that I was mourning the loss of my childhood.

I was eight years old when it first happened. In a strange way, I thought I was madly in love with him, and I believed the feeling was mutual. The abuse continued until I was 17, and even then I felt he loved me. But when I finally heard him confess, the full weight of my naiveté in the face of his sick actions hit me like a ton of bricks.

Telling my story to a detective was probably the hardest thing I have ever done, but hearing the abuser confessing was even worse. In the end, it was exactly what I needed, and God knew that. To be able to describe in detail the damage my heart and body had endured, I had to rely completely on Jesus. I sought Him deeply and proclaimed His truth about me. I was a beautiful human being – His work of art – and I needed to speak up for myself.

While facing the awful truth was excruciating, I also felt validated. I was not crazy; I didn't make it up. It did happen, and the emotions I have been experiencing were reasonable and justified.

But those feelings of exoneration were fleeting, as the pain was so great. I went back to stuffing my emotions in my shattered internal bottle, and now there were more intense emotions to tamp down. In the process, I experienced more damage. I was negative and snappy; I was broken and aching. I wanted so badly to be healed, but felt I was too damaged to be restored.

But God continued to show Himself to me daily in ways that I shouldn't have been able to deny, but I did. I turned my face and looked to the pain in my heart instead of to the joy that Jesus held out for me to grasp.

There were days that I could feel his warm embrace, yet I felt I had to fix my mess before reaching for his perfection. But He continued to show me that he desired my mess so that I could be used to give others hope in the midst of devastation. But I continued to try and fix it myself.

Eventually Jesus broke through the caverns of my soul in a miraculous way. He told me I am his masterpiece: that I have been made new and that my life should be full of joy and peace instead of sorrow and despair. I suddenly realized how much He loves me. I finally heard what He was trying to tell me all along. He has forgiven me for trying to fix myself instead of opening myself to His healing. My desire to live in despair is completely washed away. I am filled with peace and joy and with a desire to truly live instead of just walking through life.

I used to feel this was out of my reach because of all that I had done and what had been done to me. I ran from the truth because I was afraid it wouldn't be my truth, and I couldn't deal with that rejection. But through God Bumps, I realized that Jesus chose us; He gives us the option to indulge in his grace, love, and forgiveness. But it is 100% our choice. When I finally made that choice, I was restored and redeemed. My message to you is that, if you allow Him into your life, no matter what has happened in the past, you will also be restored. You are loved. You are cherished. You will be redeemed.

Denise Rossi

Chapter 15

God is Real

*"She clearly felt that God had listened
to our prayers for her."*

What does God Bumps mean to me? God Bumps are
those times in life when I am overcome by emotion and
love because He has shown me, through His Word and
Mercy, what an awesome God we serve.

I was raised in a home where my parents taught us that
our most important accomplishment is to help others
have a personal relationship with our God by showing
His love in our lives. I have made so many mistakes and
have at times walked away from God. But He has never
walked away from me and gently (usually) guides me
back. When I was a child, I wanted to be a missionary. I
have not gone overseas, but He has opened doors for me
to witness to people in my everyday life many times.

I grew up with a friend I will call MKL. She was raised
in a home where God's love was not taught. In fact, she
really did not have any time for Christians or God in her
life. Things have not been easy for her. She lost her only
sibling when he was killed in a motorcycle accident at
the age of 21. She had battled breast cancer 28 years
ago and now, unfortunately, it had returned. She was

devastated and afraid.

When MKL told me about her diagnosis, we cried together. I said I would pray that her PET scan would come back showing the cancer had not metastasized. Her response was, "Yeah, go ahead, but I don't really think it will do any good." But I was determined to do what I could to help her.

I called friends and family asking for prayers, not only for God's blessing on her health, but also for healing and softening of her heart. It was a long two weeks, but finally the PET scan results came back. We were thrilled to hear that the cancer was caught early, and it had not spread. Surgery would rid her body of the cancer without chemo or radiation.

We spent a few minutes crying, laughing and hugging. Tearfully, I said, "Thank you, Lord, and Praise God for answering our prayers!" Much to my surprise, this time her response was: "Thank you for praying for me."

That was a God Bump moment for me. I knew God had been able to use my love for Him and my faith in His mercy to reach MKL. She clearly felt that God had listened to our prayers for her. Her heart was opened to experience that God is real and that He loves us more than we can possibly understand.

Vicki Aultman

Chapter 16

Blessed Mama

*"The one thing that never wavered
was what makes me who I am
- the qualities God placed in my heart."*

God Bumps.......when I first thought of what this phrase means to me, I thought of descriptive words. Words like radiance, phenomenal, and life-changing. Although fitting, none quite matched the description of what I have experienced. In giving it more thought, I realized God Bumps are so much more than just words. They are a feeling. They are a whole-body experience!

God Bumps create different sensations with different situations. They are sometimes raised bumps on my skin where the hair on my arms is standing straight up and I feel tingly, as I realize in the moment that God is right there with me. It is just palpable. They can also be like the calm that comes over your body in a moment of pure clarity and peace in the midst of a stress-filled, tense situation.

As far back as I can remember, all I ever really wanted was to be a mom. The vision changed many times over the years. I started out wanting to be an unmarried mother to 12 children who ran an orphanage (this was during my "boys have cooties" years). That morphed

85

into having fewer children but being a stay-at-home mom married to the perfect man. He would go to his full-time job, and I would care for the children, getting them all perfectly ready and off to school. I would busy myself with daily baking and cooking, everything done before the children got home. They would bring all the neighborhood kids over for healthy homemade snacks and outside games. Of course, I was also the head of the PTO, a soccer league mom, and girl and Boy Scout leader.

As I was dreaming of what I was going to be, I changed my mind often, as most people do. The one thing that never wavered was what makes me who I am - the qualities God placed in my heart. I believe those qualities are compassion, empathy, and soft-hearted kindness for all, which grew and shined through more brightly as the years passed. I was never the straight-A-student, the popular girl or the extrovert, but always the sweet, generous, giving kid, who took the time to help and build up others.

Not only did my vision for the future begin to change and shift, but it also expanded for the better. I realized it would be great to be a mom AND a teacher. I gave a lot of thought to being a speech pathologist, working in a field where people really needed me. The idea of working with people of varying abilities became a huge passion. In high school and early college, this became my dream profession and my career goal. As the years progressed, it developed in detail. I wanted to be a special education teacher. I was ready! This was what

I was called to do in my life. I could feel it! The God Bumps told me this was it! I KNEW without a doubt God said this was it!

Yet even though I knew this was what I was meant to do, it terrified me. I was scared; I doubted myself; and I let those fears start slowing me down. Maybe I wasn't ready; maybe I couldn't do this job. I didn't feel qualified. After taking classes and working through the required college credits, I lost my drive. The dream was there, but the passion to finish the schooling was drowned out by self-doubt. I prayed; I cried; I did a lot of soul searching. I decided to stop my schooling for a short time after completing my general studies classes. I obtained an associate degree, and I would just have to be satisfied for now. Maybe I would finish my classes for teaching special education later, but something just told me to stop.

So, what did I do? I got married, and we couldn't wait to have a family! Time passed: first months, and then a year, with no results. We finally reached out to doctors and were told that I had a severe thyroid problem. We learned that getting pregnant would be complicated, and I went through painful fertility testing.

Eventually all the heartache paid off! On New Year's Eve 2001, we learned that I was pregnant with our son. After a complicated delivery, a seemingly healthy baby boy was born on August 28, 2002. But something wasn't right. We got worried when our son did not make his milestones on time, such as speech. I was doing everything a mom could for her baby, but I felt like I wasn't good enough. We got him into speech therapy and things improved some. When our son turned two, he was diagnosed with autism.

In November 2003, my father passed away somewhat unexpectedly. He had Scleroderma, which we knew would probably take his life someday. But we had no idea it would be so soon. I was a daddy's girl, and we grieved the loss of the man who was always my hero and my family's rock. I felt numb and somewhat ill, but I thought that was to be expected with the death of a loved one. Surprisingly however, two weeks after my father's funeral, we learned I was pregnant. Wow! No painful tests needed this time! We were going to have another baby. God knew just what our family needed!

This news gave us a reason to keep moving forward in our lives. We had to take care of each other because we had another baby on the way. I envisioned my Heavenly Father and my earthly father together, rocking my soon-to-be baby girl. I was overwhelmed with joy, knowing that my dad got to hold and know my daughter before she was born. God Bumps! What an amazing miracle to experience at such a sorrowful time. It was beautiful!

The birth of our daughter was challenging, frightening and miraculous all at once. How could all of that come wrapped up in one tiny bundle of baby joy? It started normally as they induced my labor, and we prepared for her birth. But in a flash, the umbilical cord dropped down before the baby, causing the cord to be wrapped around her neck. I was rushed immediately to the operating room for a C-section. As they prepped me for surgery, it all seemed surreal. I was in excruciating pain, but very aware of my surroundings, as I was concerned about the wellbeing of my baby. Time seemed to stand still. The commotion in the room was high energy with people on all sides barking orders quickly.

Suddenly, it seemed as if you could hear a pin drop. The doctors stopped, and the room went silent. The umbilical cord had gone back up, and the doctors couldn't explain it. What had just happened? No C-section needed. She entered the world of her own accord. With the cord still around her neck, she was whisked away by doctors and nurses to be checked over. Stunned by the events that just happened, my physician informed me that she had NEVER had a situation like this. What started as a frightening medical emergency turned into a win-win situation, with both mother and baby going home together happy and healthy. "You had an angel with you and that baby today," she said. The God Bumps appeared all over my body. "I do," I said, "It was my earthly and heavenly papas watching over their girls!"

While she seemed healthy, our daughter also missed a few early milestones like her older brother. She had delayed speech, low muscle tone, and in between the ages of four and five years old experienced two grand mal seizures. She was diagnosed with epilepsy, and we started doctoring in Bismarck, Fargo and Children's Hospital in Minneapolis/St Paul. At 13, after years of seeing specialist after specialist, she also was diagnosed with cerebral palsy. The cause was more than likely a birth injury, they said. We still work vigilantly with physicians in both North Dakota and Minnesota. She has her struggles, but she is an amazing kiddo who knows the meaning of hard work. She has a heart of gold and always gives 100 percent.

In 2007 we welcomed our second son to our family - the perfect baby to make our family complete. My doctor was worried from the get-go. She planned a C-section this time around, and I was very happy with that. The pregnancy and birth of our last child went well and was thankfully normal and uneventful (other than being two weeks early and still weighing in at 10 lbs., 14oz.). It was obvious in his early months that he was also delayed in milestones. Due to the diagnoses of his siblings, it was no question to the doctors or us as parents that he was possibly on the autism spectrum. Although a clinical diagnosis did not come until he was 18 months old, we lost no time getting early interventions for him.

However, trying to navigate the confusing system of getting help for three special-needs children, medical bills, therapy appointments and demanding schedules added a strain to our marriage that we were not equipped to handle. No time together as a couple left us exhausted, caused hurt and moved us further and further apart. My husband struggled to accept the autism diagnoses and the thought of HIS children being "different" from others, causing pain and anger. He absolutely loved his children, but was overwhelmed by guilt, that perhaps something in his genetics was responsible for causing these issues. He was tormented by the what ifs and whys.

In August 2011, our 11-year marriage ended. The ending was marked with great sadness, pain and an incredible sense of loss. We remained friends, but I felt broken and very alone. Suddenly, I had to transition from a stay-at-home mom to a mom who needed to be in the workforce while raising three children who needed me more than ever. I wasn't sure if I could do it. I prayed and prayed, "Lord, please show me the way. Show me what am I to do." And He did!

The baby of the family was now starting preschool part-time, and one day I was asked if I would like to work there as a lunch supervisor! It was perfect because it would only be on the days that the kids were in school. I was excited yet nervous as I hadn't worked outside of the home for years. But I followed God's lead and made a giant leap of faith.

Fast forward to the present day: I have been a single mom for more than nine years. The kids and I live on our own in a house with our dog and three bunnies. I now work full time as a paraprofessional in special education in the same school where I started as a lunch supervisor. Life is complicated and hectic, crazy with routine after routine dominating our days, not leaving much room for anything spontaneous. But life for our family is happy, beautiful, and amazing. We find joy in not only the big things, but also in what others would find typical, ordinary, and mundane, and would take for granted.

My conclusions about God Bumps. They are:

• What I get daily when I realize the blessings I have in my life, and what I feel because I know that God has more in store for me in this life.

• The way I feel when I think about the gift of motherhood God gave me. He has the faith, belief in and love for me that no earthly being ever could. He trusts me to care for, unconditionally love and protect three of His precious children.

• How I feel when I realize that He CHOSE me to be the mother of these children! He chose me and shaped me into the person, and then into the mother, He wanted for them.

I was never meant to be a speech pathologist or a teacher. I was meant to be a mom to three amazing children with differing needs who teach me something every day. I was meant to help other children by using the knowledge I have gained from having my own. I have learned more about life, happiness, perseverance, courage, patience, understanding and the true meaning of love from them than I could have ever learned in school. They are my heroes and my inspiration in this life. They have made me a better mom and a better person.

In hindsight, God always had HIS plan. He molded me

into who I am: with my soft heart, empathy, strong will, and passion for children and those with differing abilities. Through all the years of schooling and dreaming of working with children with special needs, He was shaping me to fulfill that plan. It was the dream He had for my life the whole time! I am one blessed mama!

Renee Hardy

Chapter 17

A Beautiful Gift From God

"As I began praying, he lifted the arm I was not holding and began to point and said, 'Look...'"

To me, God Bumps are when I get chills down my spine and bumps on my arms and legs, and feel a warm, peaceful presence when reading or talking about God, or sometimes just in prayer.

There was a God Bump moment that really touched my heart and changed my life, as well as how I view the Holy Catholic Mass. It started one Saturday morning after early Mass. My cousin came up to me and said that our uncle was in the hospital and did not have much time left to live. I decided to go see him, and when I entered the hospital room, I was pleased to see that he was awake. He asked me to pray for him, and I said I would. I was thinking that after I left I would go to the chapel and pray, but I soon realized he wanted me to pray for him at that moment.

I sat next to him, took his hand, and began to pray silently, the Chaplet of Divine Mercy. As I began praying, he lifted the arm I was not holding and began to point

94

and said, "Look…" He was seeing his family that had preceded him in death and was saying their names. I got chills down my spine and felt a warm, beautiful presence all around me and my uncle. That was the last I saw of my uncle in this world, as he passed away shortly after that.

Two weeks later something amazing happened when I went to Sunday morning Mass. After receiving Holy Communion, I knelt to pray. Suddenly, I was blessed with a vision of my uncle. He was coming toward me, along with my dad, my mom, and many others who preceded him in death. I began to weep, feeling so overwhelmed that God allowed me to receive such a beautiful gift. Not only had I received Jesus His Son, but it seemed as if I had received a glimpse of Heaven. For quite some time after that, I could feel the warmth of that moment, of feeling His loving, peaceful presence deep within me. It was a beautiful gift that I will never forget.

Jerome Volk

Chapter 18

Sleep in Havenly Peace, Momma Bear

"God truly knows all. He had this planned, and little did we know that this night truly was a God-given night."

It amazes me that as humans we may not be able to remember what we had for lunch, but other things we can remember precisely even though they happened years ago. There is one particular night that I will never, ever forget. I think that's because the entire night was filled with God Bumps – what I call those "God touched me" moments.

It was Christmas Eve 2001, and my children and I were getting ready to open gifts. Our holiday celebration was interrupted by the telephone ringing. I answered it and was happy to hear it was one of my sisters, thinking she had called to wish us a Merry Christmas. But my happiness quickly changed to concern because she was calling to tell me to come to the hospital as soon as I possibly could. Our mother had taken a turn for the worse, and it didn't look like she was going to live much longer.

Mom had been sick off and on for a few years. She had double hip replacement, multiple mini strokes, and a massive heart attack. My dad was a trooper and had been her caregiver through all that, but she had been in the hospital for the past couple months. For some reason though, I never really thought about her dying. I guess I just wanted to hang on to my mom or as we called her, Momma Bear. I couldn't imagine a world without her.

We opened our gifts quickly, and my daughter and I took off for the hospital - about 140 miles away. I was praying to get there in time to say good-bye to Mom. I remember clearly that our drive was so beautiful. At one point, we were driving through a wildlife refuge, and I was worried about hitting critters crossing the road. But there was a very bright and peaceful light that was behind us, seeming to be shining just for us. When I turned my head, I couldn't see it; but when I looked forward, it lit the road as far as I could see. I knew this light was not just the moon, but it was a guiding light from God. He answered my prayer for safe travels and to get to the hospital before my mom passed.

I have four sisters and three brothers, and my sister from California had come home to visit. My dad had been spending every moment of every day he could with Mom in the hospital. To get Dad out and about, my brother-in-law asked him if he wanted to go to the farm where my brother-in-law and sister lived. Dad agreed it would be good to take a little break, so off he went.

At the hospital, my daughter, my three sisters and I hugged, cried and gathered around Mom. I sat on her right side and held her hand, the same hand I held as a child. I looked at her beautiful hand, worn from hard work, usually warm, but now cool to the touch. I thought of all the things she did with those hands in her life. I remember the big, bountiful vegetable garden she raised and her tending her beautiful flower gardens with those hands. I remember the games of cards and board games that she used to play with those hands. I remember the endless hours she spent canning the goods from the garden, so we'd have good eats all winter, and the baking she did was unbelievably delicious. And the hugs, the touch on the shoulder...so many memories of this woman I call Mom are now instilled in me.

God truly knows all. He had this planned, and little did we know that this night truly was a God-given night. Surely God knew that Mom's favorite day of the year was Christmas Eve. She loved it because the family she loved so dearly would all be under her roof at home. We would eat the goods that Mom made: Norwegian Krumkake, Fattigmann, Rosettes, and so much more. Mom loved her coffee and sweets - so delish! We would listen to our favorite Christmas carols, and especially Mom's favorite song, "Silent Night." Our little record player had to be plugged in and warmed up before it would play the LP. I still have that record player and the records Mom used to play during the Christmas season: oh, the memories.

Time was drawing nigh, and we could tell Mom was having a hard time hanging on. It was shortly after

9 p.m. and Mom's breaths were becoming more of a struggle. With her hand in mine and knowing God's love for her, I looked at her and said, "It's okay Mom, you can go home." The television had been on softly in the background. At that moment, we heard a country artist start singing "Silent Night." As our beautiful mother breathed her last breath, we heard him sing, "Sleep in heavenly peace." The moment Mom passed, I felt that she was floating above all of us in the room. She was radiant, no sickness, no troubles – she was free of her earthly burdens. I know without a doubt that God opened the gates of Heaven for her.

Shortly after her passing, Dad and my brother-in-law came back from the farm. Dad realized what had just happened and broke down and cried. I'd never seen my dad cry before. I wanted to hug him but let him have his space. We all left the room so Dad could be with Mom. I felt in my heart that Mom didn't want Dad to see her pass and had waited for him to leave so he wouldn't have to see her take her last breath.

Dad was a firm man but had a big, mushy heart. I remember him trying to hug mom and swing her around while she was working in the kitchen. Mom would use her Norwegian words now and then and said, "Don't you have something better to do?" She loved dad's attention but was more private that way. They had a very special relationship.

Mom, just months earlier, had written on a piece of paper, "Happy 20002." And she wrote it just like that, even though the upcoming year would be 2002. Did she know something we didn't know? While visiting my parents, I had seen it hanging on the refrigerator through the course of the few months. It seemed strange it was 20002 instead of 2002 but that's what she wrote. Could it be that she was thinking about eternity, rather than just the New Year? Was she trying to tell us that time is infinite, and whatever we are experiencing right now is but a blip? Was she trying to tell us that everything will be all right, whether it's 2002 or 20002?

One summer weekend after Mom passed away, I went home to check in on Dad. He was managing, but it was hard for him without Mom. The country-sized yard needed some grooming, as did the flower gardens. I was trying to weed one flower garden that was nearly impossible because of all the overgrowth. I was feeling a little overwhelmed with all that needed to be done.

As I was sitting on the sidewalk looking at what used to be a beautiful flower garden, a butterfly landed on my shoulder. It was beautiful; I think it was a Monarch butterfly. At first, I thought nothing of it, but it would not go away. Then I said, "Mom, is that you?" I believe this was a sign from God and from Mom. She was telling me not to worry about what was. We sat in silence, and after a few minutes, she flew away. I did not worry about the garden and just did some soil turning to get at the biggest weeds. I knew it was okay just the way it was…because mom said so. After I did what I could, I went into the house and spent time with Dad. That was more important than cleaning out the garden.

What a wonderful blessing from above, and I carry that message still today in my heart.

God does work in mysterious ways, and He is always ready to hand out those God Bump moments. We just need to open our hearts and be ready to experience them.

Gail Withey

Chapter 19

Picture Perfect

"When I walked into his office, the first thing I saw was the identical picture of Christ and the police car that I had in my office in Concordia. I mentioned it to him and he said, 'You will be the next...'"

As we reflect on our lives, we often see that God has opened doors or helped us map things out. God does not control our choices as though we are puppets but allows us free will to make choices. But it is key to recognize signals that will keep us on the road designed by God. Taking a side road can lead to separation from God or the loss of opportunities to serve Him.

I believe that God wants us to have a fulfilling life and be spiritually alive. Too often our personal moral compasses point us in the wrong direction. We must learn to depend on God and pray for good direction and discernment. Many times, I have been able to trace a decision-making event to a spiritual connection. However, one particularly stands out to be more revealing.

In 1985, I was working as the Chief of Police in Concordia, Kansas, with a population of 8,000. I had two years of college and was also teaching at a junior college.

I was interested in relocating to a larger community, especially one that had a four-year college. But so far, nothing had come up. We liked Concordia and had family and good friends there. The sheriff and I were great friends, and we had an excellent working relationship. He had a picture in his office that I liked. It was an oil painting depicting Christ with arms outspread over a police car during a rainstorm. I mentioned how much I admired that picture, and when he retired, he gave it to me. That meant a lot to me, and I proudly displayed it in my office.

In October of that year, my wife and I attended an International Chiefs of Police Convention in Houston, Texas. There were hundreds of vendors displaying the latest in police equipment or whose business promoted criminal justice programs and events. As we walked among the vendors, my wife stopped at the "Adam-12" booth. Stars from this popular 1970s TV show were making an appearance. I was standing next to a booth that advertised colleges offering criminal justice programs. I picked up a pamphlet to read while waiting for my wife. It opened to a page with an employment ad for a Chief of Police in Mandan, North Dakota.

The ad indicated that nearby, in Bismarck, North Dakota, Mary College offered four-year degrees. It piqued my interest, so I picked up the pamphlet and took it home. When I asked my wife what she thought, her first comment was that we did not know anyone there and have never even been to North Dakota. But she told me to go ahead and send in a resume and application. We both thought it unlikely that I would be considered. We went about our lives and forgot about the application until on one January day I got a call from the auditor in Mandan. I was shocked when he said that I was one of the three top finalists being considered for the chief's position. However, both other applicants had four-year degrees and were working in larger departments.

The auditor said they would provide an airline ticket to fly into Mandan for an interview and fly out the following morning. I said I preferred to take some time checking out the people and the community. My wife and I drove to Mandan (700 miles) and spent several days there prior to the interview. We explored the area, went to the Chamber of Commerce, and viewed other key parts of the town.

One important stop was a visit with the local sheriff, as I knew from experience that it was critical to have a good relationship between the sheriff and the chief of police. When I walked into his office, the first thing I saw was the identical picture of Christ and the police car that I had in my office in Concordia. I mentioned it to him, and he said, "You will be the next Chief of Police in Mandan."

Before we got back to Concordia, I was notified that I was the person selected for the job. This was a difficult decision for us, as our roots were in Kansas. We would be strangers in Mandan, not knowing anyone very well. Our oldest son and daughter, along with a grandson, lived in Kansas and we would be leaving them and other family members behind. Our youngest was graduating from high school and joining the army. My wife would have to stay in Concordia for at least three months before she could join me in Mandan, as my job would begin March 1st.

After praying and giving full thought to the situation, we decided to accept the job in Mandan. The picture of Christ and the police car was like a traffic signal light that turned green, signaling the "go" sign. To this day, I have never seen anything resembling that painting anywhere else.

Looking back over the last 30 years, God has greatly blessed us in our decision to relocate. My work as police chief has been a good experience. I also was ordained as a deacon, taught religion classes to junior high students, worked in community and church events and made many good friends. We were fortunate to have grandchildren and great-grand children stay with us at times. Our daughter and her husband now live in Mandan. We also have a grandson, his wife and a great-granddaughter living nearby.

My advice is to look to God for guidance, pray, and be aware when God opens a door. It is up to us to walk through it. You never know what blessings are waiting on the other side.

Deacon Dennis Rohr

Chapter 20

Time Stood Still

"God had given me an answer."

Early on the morning of April 19, 2013, I was startled awake when my phone rang. It was my brother-in-law, who lived just down the street from me. He said he was in my driveway, so I quickly got up, put on my robe, and went to let him in.

I knew something was very wrong for him to be there at that time of the morning. My first thought was that our mother, who was up in age, had passed away. Instead, he gave me the horrific news that my son had passed away that morning from an apparent heart attack. He was only 44, which is the same age that his father was when he died from a heart attack.

My son had died at home sometime during the night. His wife found him lying on the floor when she got up to make his coffee. There was one nagging question for me: what time had my son actually passed away? The coroner couldn't give us a definite time. As a mother, it bothered me that I didn't know when my child left this world.

We got through the funeral and spent the next week

with family. When we got home, I noticed that the clock in our living room had stopped at 12:35, but the clock was not run down. I got it started, but that night it stopped again at 12:35. This happened for the next three nights. Finally, it dawned on me that God was telling me that was the time my son had passed. After I came to that realization, I felt a weight being lifted from my shoulders. Since that day, the clock never stopped again and continues to run to this day.

God had given me an answer, and I feel that answer has helped me deal with the grief that I've experienced.

Ruth Seehafer

Chapter 21

Blessings in Disguise

"I've gone from a person who had no real connection with God to a person who reads Scripture and prays every day – and so does my son."

If I have learned anything in life, it is that God has a plan for each of us. We may encounter some twists and turns along the way, but if we trust in Him, everything will turn out OK. We discover that those God Bumps on life's journey are actually blessings in disguise. Having said that, it would appear that I have been richly blessed with bumps in the road! I grew up in Washington, where my dad had gone to find work. My parents were both out-of-control alcoholics, and I was the youngest of six children. I have memories of spending time in foster care and that our foster mother was mean.

As a result of this tough childhood, I spent much of my adolescence drinking and partying heavily. Fortunately, God intervened at that time, and I ended up moving to North Dakota to live with my grandmother. This God Bump was one of the best things that ever happened to me. I wasn't a practicing Christian at the time, but He was always there for me.

I ended up working as a bartender, where I met Kevin. He was attractive and was a scrapper, but I didn't fall for him right away. In fact, we argued when he came into the bar, so I assumed he didn't like me. But one day he left a note on my car asking to see me, and soon I was head over heels in love.

But there were problems. In my mind, love was followed by marriage and family. You committed to each other and took care of each other. But Kevin didn't see it that way. He said he never wanted to get married...Ever...To anyone. It was apparently something he had also heard from his father – don't ever get married. So, against my better judgment, I moved in with Kevin. We were together for four years when I learned I was expecting a baby.

Kevin was very upset when I got pregnant, but I was excited. Wyatt was born in December 1992, and I was thrilled. I loved having a son! But Kevin was bitter and didn't help with Wyatt very much. Then later I learned Wyatt had ADHD, which complicated matters.

Things went from bad to worse, and Kevin started seeing another woman. She resented Wyatt and me, especially any money that went toward our support. Soon after, he told us to move out. It was Father's Day 1994.

I was crushed and scared. I didn't know where to go or what I was going to do. I had one sibling in the state, so I packed Wyatt up and went to my brother Dave's house. The Lord was working on a plan for us, and I am so grateful that Dave agreed to take us in. That was a definite God Bump moment. Dave lives on a farm in the central part of the state. I managed to find work at a nursing home in a neighboring town, and I helped Dave milk cows and make hay for their feed.

We had been staying with my brother for six months when another God Bump moment happened. A couple that had been renting a home nearby was moving and asked me if I would be interested in renting it. It was on 30 acres, which was absolutely perfect because Wyatt's ADHD was becoming more evident, and this would give him lots of room to run around. We took it, and it was a great move for us.

I used a local professional for my income taxes, and I mentioned to her that I like numbers. One day she said she had a proposition for me. She was getting ready to retire and was looking for someone to buy her business. She asked me if I would be interested - another God Bump moment! In my wildest dreams, I had never pictured myself being in the income tax business. But I knew God had a plan for me, so I jumped in with both feet, trained for two years, took some college courses, and then took over the business in 2009. It was a Godsend for Wyatt and me. We were able to get past the feeling of being financially strapped all the time and were able to do some fun things.

Kevin's relationship with Wyatt over the years has been bumpy. In the early years, Kevin's mom insisted that he see Wyatt and accused me of keeping them apart. That wasn't true as Kevin never really tried to see him. In the last few years, however, they have made their relationship work. Wyatt has figured out how to handle Kevin, and I decided to leave the past behind us, so we get along fine. I never got married, and my business has kept me busy. I love traveling in my spare time. Wyatt is grown now and has a full-time job. ADHD keeps him on the move all the time, but he is handling it.

When Kevin kicked us out, I was at one of the lowest points in my life. In hindsight, it's clear that through the grace of God I dodged a bullet when that relationship ended. I've gone from a person who had no real connection with God to a person who reads Scripture and prays every day – and so does my son. God has shown me that He has a plan for each of us, that all we need to do is trust in our Creator. We may experience bumps along the road, but if we think of them as God Bumps that are often blessings in disguise, our faith will one day make it clear that our path leads straight to Him.

Cathy Hill

Chapter 22

Angel of God

***"I know deep in my heart that my beautiful boy
was saved by his guardian angel that day."***

God Bumps are real; they confirm that God is with
us and always will be. To me it means that there is no
explanation for something that happens other than
through God's divine assistance.

My first-born son, Derek, had a challenging beginning in
life. Because of complications, he was born at 27 weeks.
The circumstances of his birth were a miracle in itself.
Because of amniotic fluid leaking and the umbilical
cord wrapped around his neck, he never should have
survived this life. God, on the other hand, must have
wanted him to be with us.

Derek was small, only 2 lbs. when he was born, but he
was a good patient. His weight eventually went up to
4 lbs., 6 oz., two months after his birth. We were then
able to bring him home from the hospital with an apnea
machine. We were absolutely thrilled, but nervous at
the same time. There were challenges, but Derek was a
happy and mostly healthy child.

Fast forward to age three. Derek was also a curious

child, and he liked to "help" his mom and dad around the house. Our home was designed with the basement steps in the center of the house. The basement was unfinished, and we had a door at the top of the steps that was typically closed. There was no handrail or any kind of protection on either side of the steps.

One fateful day, my husband Darryl had gone downstairs to work on something. Derek followed him to "help" his dad. When the project was done, they went upstairs with Derek leading. When at the top, Darryl realized he hadn't shut a light off. He turned around and went back down. Unbeknownst to Darryl, Derek tried to follow him and fell from the top step down. His fall was about seven feet, and he landed on the bare concrete floor.

Panic ensued, and we rushed Derek to the emergency room. How could this have happened? The tears flowed, and we prayed that he would be all right. Thankfully, the news was good. He did have a large bump on his head, but the doctor said he would be ok. We were advised to keep an eye on him, and everything seemed to be all right. Hallelujah!

About a year later, Darryl and I were at the kitchen table talking, and he said, "I still remember when Derek fell off the steps and how we couldn't believe he wasn't hurt worse than he was."

Derek overheard us and came running from the playroom. He said, "I remember that! It was soft when I landed."

We looked at each other, and I said to Derek, "It couldn't have been soft, you landed on concrete." But something told me to probe a little more, so I asked him, "What do you mean? What did it feel like?"

Much to our surprise, Derek said, "You know like when you land on a pillow or something soft - like feathers."

We couldn't believe what we were hearing! When we could finally speak, I said, "Oh my goodness, Derek that was your guardian angel."

I know deep in my heart that my beautiful boy was saved by his guardian angel that day. No one will ever convince me otherwise. That was one of my God Bump moments. God is with us and always will be. He certainly was with Derek that day, and we will be eternally grateful!

Melanie Korezak

Chapter 23

Everything Matters

"He was attempting to satiate his thirst for the Lord, while I was attempting to put a better trajectory on my drives and learing to putt with more confidence and a steadier hand."

To me a God Bump is when we encounter a nudge, a message through those we encounter or an event that is unmistakably from God. When something occurs, we immediately know it is out of the ordinary. We know it is from God.

Everything matters. Do not diminish the impact of each encounter you have, regardless of how inconsequential it may appear at the time. A few years ago, I casually bumped into an acquaintance at a conference sponsored by my church diocese. He said that the more he is exposed to information about our faith, the greater is his desire for more. He described it as a thirst, and I sensed this thirst in him. It was a thirst for the Lord, a thirst to know more about our faith through the many resources we have. Whether it is scripture, CDs, books, Catholic radio or other materials available to enlighten our minds, they help feed our souls and advance our journey with and to the Lord. He mentioned our new, local Catholic radio station that I had not listened to yet.

At the time, most of my casual reading was on materials designed to improve my golf game – everything from the ideal state of mind to striking my irons with authority and accuracy. I focused a lot of energy on putting accuracy, along with developing, implementing and perfecting that beautiful, elusive power draw off the tee box with a driver.

My friend did not go out of his way to evangelize me, and I am sure he left the conversation not knowing he had made an impact on me. He was merely making heartfelt conversation. But his words caused me to do a double take, a real self-evaluation. His spare time was spent pursuing the Lord. He was attempting to satiate his thirst for the Lord, while I was attempting to put a better trajectory on my drives and learning to putt with more confidence and a steadier hand. It gave me pause.

The conference offered complimentary copies of the Magnificat, a monthly publication containing scripture readings for morning and evening. Also included weredaily scriptures used in weekday Mass, along with a meditation for the day and a short bio on the saint of the day. I had not been aware that such a publication existed. I took it home, and the next Monday I read the morning reading for the day and went to noon Mass. I continued with daily Mass and expanded to weekly adoration, accompanied by the Rosary and Chaplet of Divine Mercy.

I remember thinking after my first adoration that I had just had the most real experience of my life. My experience on the effects of daily Eucharist are one of slow transformation where the fruits of the Holy Spirit gradually take root, develop and grow: love, joy, peace, patience, kindness, goodness, faithfulness, gentleness and self-control. The fruits of the Holy Spirit help one to become a better husband, father, worker, golf teammate, co-worker, brother, uncle, neighbor, friend, parishioner and member of the community.

The next step was to rediscover the precious gift of the sacrament of Reconciliation. To confess one's sins, to repent, to ask for forgiveness and receive forgiveness is a transforming gift beyond description. I have come to learn that everything comes at a price, and that the Son of God paid the ultimate price. He made the ultimate sacrifice out of love for us, His children. The Sacrament of Reconciliation has given me the gift of gratitude. I feel deep gratitude to God for His gift of forgiveness, for the gift of life, and for the many blessings He has bestowed and continues to bestow on me and my family every day.

I once again had a chance encounter with the same acquaintance at a business function four months later. I mentioned that I had tuned into that radio station and was now listening exclusively to Catholic radio. He then invited me to attend a local men's group that meets at one of our parishes every Tuesday morning at 6:30 a.m. The group reads books pertinent to our faith and then meets to discuss the assigned pages for the week. I was shocked to discover the depth, substance and faith of this group of more than 20 men in our community. Meeting with these men every Tuesday morning keeps me on track in my faith journey and provides a sounding board for questions or reflections I may have. These men are a wonderful source of knowledge and inspiration for me.

Three years ago, I was approached by a parishioner after daily Mass inquiring if I would be interested in a three-day weekend at a Jesuit retreat house. He had made 26 of these annual retreats and highly recommended the experience. I agreed, have attended for the fourth year in a row. The retreats are a great way to decelerate, refocus and get closer to God.

My faith journey over these past few years could be described as a "domino" effect of God Bumps. What started as a casual conversation has led to blossoming of my faith and a thirst for the Father, the Son and the Holy Spirit. My friend did not intentionally evangelize that day. Just by being himself and sharing his story, he made a significant impact on my life. He led me to take the next step, which led to the next, which led to the next. Everything matters. Everything we do. Everything we say. Every encounter we have every day. You never know where or when the next God Bump in your life or someone else's may occur. Everything matters because we matter to God.

SLW

Chapter 24

My God Bumps Moment

"Prior to having a relationship with God, I was a lost woman, going the wrong direction FAST! I was a drug addict on a sure-fire track to destruction. On the brink of losing my two children, I was looking at jail time."

If you were to ask me what God Bumps are, I would tell you that it is when God moves in your life in such a way that you know with absolute certainty it can only be Him. When God shows up and shows off! For me, there is no better way to describe it.

I have had many instances in my life where God has done just that. However, the one that I want to share is the day that God restored me to Himself. That was a miracle.

Prior to having a relationship with God, I was a lost woman, going the wrong direction FAST! I was a drug addict on a sure-fire track to destruction. On the brink of losing my two children, I was looking at jail time. If I continued on that path, I believe I most likely would have died.

But God came into my life and, in one moment, changed me from the inside out. He showed me that, above all else,

He loved me. There was nothing that I needed to do to win His love, He just did it.

After spending nearly six years lost in addiction, my boyfriend (now husband) and I walked into a local church. I had been there before, but this time was different. We listened to the message and immediately knew that God was calling us to something more. Although we didn't know what it was at the time, we knew it was freedom from what we had been living. We accepted the call and gave our lives over to the Lord.

That was my God Bump. From that very moment, God began a work in us that we could not have done on our own. I believe it was the work of redemption. Drugs had stolen everything from me, but God was redeeming me. He took me from the miry clay and set my feet on the Rock that is His Son, Jesus Christ. He gave me a new name better than any name I had before. He showed me that if I were the only person in the world, He still would have sent His Son to die on the Cross for me.

I no longer walk this world chained to addiction or wrong living, instead have been redeemed by the Creator of all things. He chose me!! I went from a homeless, hopeless woman of the world to a woman of God, filled with hope for the future. There is no greater joy than to know we are walking in truth. From that God Bump moment to today, I know with absolute certainty that God worked a miracle. He saved me.

Deborah Withey

Chapter 25

In the Garden

"We believe God chose that one particular moment, when He knew we were struggling greatly for comfort and hope, to give us that little God Bump that said, 'I am here, and I will never leave your side. You will get through this.'"

What is a God Bump? To me, it is a little gift from God, reminding us He is right there by our side, no matter what trials and tribulations in life we are facing. When it seems you can't make it one more moment, these little God Bumps come to us when least expected and most needed, lifting us up, forcing us to remember what we so often forget ... He will never leave our side and has us wrapped in His arms each moment of every day.

Since losing our oldest son Cody in a tragic accident on May 15, 2016, life has been a struggle. I am sure every grieving parent feels the same way. Some days are worse than others, but by the grace of God, we find ourselves getting a little stronger each day.

One sunny morning a month after Cody's death, my husband and I were each lost in our own thoughts, trying to force ourselves to do something, anything, to take our minds off our pain, if only for a few minutes.

We had just marked our 26th wedding anniversary, but so soon after losing our son, we didn't feel like celebrating. I eventually found myself in the garden doing some weeding, and my husband followed me outside and began trimming trees. I made progress, gradually making my way into the peas. We planted peas each year, not only because we liked them, but also for our toy poodle Brandy, who was strangely obsessed with them and eagerly awaited the pea crop. They had really taken off, causing the plants to lay on their sides. I was going down the row, flipping the plants up as I went and plucking any weeds that I came across.

In the middle of the row, I flipped up one plant and could not believe my eyes! There, sticking out of the dirt and glistening in the early-morning sun, was my wedding band, which had been missing for the past eight years. I lost it in the backyard, more than likely while also weeding the garden. We borrowed my parents' metal detector shortly after I lost it and scoured the yard from top to bottom with no luck. The garden had been planted each year in the same spot and tilled up twice a year. Amazingly we never came across it – until that moment.

I started screaming, which caused my husband to drop what he was doing and run to see what was going on. He thought it was probably a snake or some other varmint that caused my reaction. When I showed him what was sticking out of the dirt, we both were speechless. We looked at each other, and both instantly teared up. We knew that we had just been given a sign.

We ended that day with our hearts a little lighter than they had been for a while. We believe God chose that one particular moment, when He knew we were struggling greatly for comfort and hope, to give us that little God Bump that said, "I am here, and I will never leave your side. You will get through this."

Missy Block

Chapter 26

The Healing Power of Jesus

"When the Lord pulled me from the precipice of death, he cleared my mind and gave me purpose. He healed me."

The Bible tells us that God will never forsake us. He has always been with me, and I know this because of the God Bumps that I've experienced. They are the special things that God does in my life that are out of the ordinary, and I get them all the time!

I didn't learn about God from my parents. Mom was Christian, but Dad only went to church on Christmas and Easter. We didn't really have any Christian leadership at home. As I got older, my cousin picked me up for Sunday night services. It was there that I began to hear about and believe in the healing power of Jesus.

My first God Bump happened when I was 14, growing up on a farm. One spring there was too much stubble left from the last year's crop, so we had to burn it off to plant the new crop. My brother and I created a fire break on one end of the area, right next to a prairie road that was just a pickup trail, not a gravel road. We started the fire from the other end, and all went according to plan – until the wind picked up. We watched in horror as the wind fanned the flames and swept across the field. As it jumped over the fire break we had created, I started praying: "God, if you will stop this fire, I will serve you." And sure enough, the fire stopped right at the pickup trail. I will never forget that feeling, and I kept my word – most of the time.

My home life as a child was rough; Dad was stubborn and had a bad temper. When I was younger, I helped him on the farm and things were ok between us. But when I became a teenager, our relationship deteriorated significantly. He didn't want to hear my opinion about anything, and we argued about everything. Even though I would have liked to work on our family farm, I left home at 16 and soon joined the military.

When I was 17, I knew I wanted to give my heart to the Lord. One Sunday night, I wanted to go up to the altar, but I was too shy to go by myself. The preacher must have recognized that because he said if some didn't want to come up alone, they should just come up when everyone else does. As I walked to the altar, I asked God to save me, and that's exactly what He did. It was the best experience of my life. He washed my sins away, and I felt as if a 2,000-lb. weight had been lifted off my chest. From then on, my life had to be different.

I served in the military during the Vietnam War, and I had the opportunity to witness to many people during my time there. I cleaned up my language and didn't party or drink. But I was just a farm boy, and despite my faith, I was plenty scared. I was overseas for nine months and 21 days and came back with no diseases, never shot anyone, and never got shot. I did a lot of praying, and I believe the Lord protected me. I felt a calling to become a minister, but I didn't follow through with it.

I married my wife Carol soon after I got out of the service. My parents didn't come to our wedding, and I didn't talk to Dad for a long time. After I got married, I strayed from God for a few years. I still went to church, but just didn't call on the Lord as I had in the past. Our marriage was rocky at times, and I'm sad to say that I verbally and emotionally abused Carol. I realized I've inherited my dad's temper and was following in his footsteps. Our pastor suggested I read a book entitled "Men in Midlife Crises," and I felt as if it was speaking directly to me. It helped me understand why I was feeling and acting the way I was. Except for the Bible, it is the best book I've ever read. Fortunately, we took our vows seriously and never divorced. We have three wonderful children. I rededicated my life to the Lord and apologized to Carol for how I acted in the past. She said she appreciated it.

My relationship with my parents also improved with the Lord's help. One day I came home from work and Dad was there. We talked for a long time and got along after that. Mom even lived with us for a while. The biggest God Bump, though, is that before Dad passed, he gave his heart to the Lord. That means everything to me.

I started having health problems and spent a lot of time at the doctor. One day I suddenly could not walk and ended up in the hospital. No one could figure out why that happened, so I was sent to a care facility for physical therapy. That didn't help, and then my kidneys started shutting down. A chemical went to my brain, and I was completely out of it for two days. Carol and my nurse sat with me day and night, as they didn't think I was going to make it.

For two days, I screamed in pain and prayed to die. I was hurting so badly that it messed with my head. I started praying for healing, and then God took over. My kidney function came back, my blood pressure went down, and my stomach started to function again. Obviously, the Lord had plans for me, and dying wasn't one of them at the time.

While I'm doing much better, I still have health issues and difficulty walking. I have moved into a care community. I hope to go home someday, but if these issues aren't corrected, I don't want Carol to have to take care of me. We talk twice a day now and discuss everything, more than we ever talked about when we lived together. We look at it this way: I am here for a reason – to witness to others and to help people have a brighter outlook. I can see God's hand working in every corner of this place. Being sick has strengthened me, and I am his vessel. When the Lord pulled me from the precipice of death, he cleared my mind and gave me purpose. He healed me.

At the age of nine, my grandson has expressed interest in becoming a preacher, and that is a big God Bump for me. The Lord also has given me a second chance to be a minister, just in a different way then I imagined back when I first heard His call. There are times when I lie in bed at night, and I feel as if God is preparing me to preach a sermon of some kind. I pray that I will have the right words at the right time for someone who needs the healing power of Jesus. Or a God Bump!

Gaylen Boeckel

Chapter 27

God's Plan Brings Bundle of Joy

*"My husband came to my workplace to tell me,
and he was crying so hard that I thougtht
something terrible had happened."*

I would describe God Bumps as the sensation that is felt upon receiving good or not very good news about things that happen in our lives. Just the other day I heard of an unfortunate situation, and I immediately said a quick prayer for the family. That is utilizing the power of prayer after feeling the sensation of God Bumps.

When Bruce and I got married in June 2009, we didn't know God's plan for us. We took a vow to have God place children within our home, and we had early on discussed adopting as a possibility. With no children yet in our lives, in 2012 we decided to make a submission to a local adoption agency, including a home study and other required documents. At first, we wanted to stay within our home state, and we played the waiting game for two years. In 2014 we asked to be placed on out-of-state adoption lists in hopes of being selected. We even took special photos and tried to organize them to look like real-life situations for a child in our loving home.

Finally, in December of 2014, we learned we had been selected! My husband came to my workplace to tell me, and he was crying so hard that I thought something terrible had happened. It was actually the direct opposite – the best news ever! He said a birth mother had chosen us, and we needed to have all the medical information cleared by our doctor within the next 24 hours. We also reviewed information with a nurse about the child's and his family's medical history and acknowledged it was something we were willing to accept.

The baby boy was due at the end of January. We gathered items for the baby's room and excitedly did all the normal things parents do while "nesting." Our son, Alex Jacob, was born February 2nd, and we were thrilled! Our prayers were answered. We didn't care if this baby was a boy or girl; we prayed for a healthy baby. We also fervently prayed that the birth mother would be at peace with her decision and be granted the strength she needed during her pregnancy and thereafter.

Alex is five years old now, and we not only thank God every day for all the love and happiness he has brought us, but also for the choice that his birth mother made: Life, a true gift from God. The Bible verse that I most relate to my life and the life of our little Alex is Isaiah 49 – "I will never forget you and never abandon you."

God has been with us whenever we have needed him. We didn't know when we got married that we couldn't have children, but God had a plan for us. Why else would we have talked about adoption at such an early stage – God Bumps! We prayed and we persisted in pursuing adoption because we knew that God would not abandon us and our desire to have children in our lives. We feel richly blessed.

Kristie Schumacher

Chapter 28

Nothing is too Big for God

"I felt angry and full of hate: hopeless, with no way out. It was time to turn to God."

I realized a God Bump years ago in a job that I once liked but had turned into a horrible experience after a big change in the company. I had been working with a talented electrical engineer "John," of Chinese ethnicity. Through that connection, I learned about the Chinese culture, which includes a great respect for one's elders, especially leaders. As a senior electronics technician engaged in many projects, I worked with John from time to time, and we worked well together.

When the big change came, John became my manager. I was moved out of my role as electronics technician into a role of designer, which was not something I did daily. These were uncomfortable changes that left many questioning our new roles and responsibilities. It was not a good time in the company.

Our upper-level leader was also Chinese, and John never questioned his decisions, which I assume was at least partly due to cultural traditions. He would just carry out those directives, but I could tell that, deep down, John did not like the changes thrust upon him either. John was no longer in the engineering role he loved and with him as my manager, our relationship also suffered. I was now asked to perform tasks I was not good at, and that were taking longer. A job that once was a joy now became absolutely agonizing, and I dreaded coming to work. John was under great pressure from above, and he transferred it to me. I found myself resenting him and his decisions. How could he do this to me when we once worked together so well? I started looking for another job. I felt angry and full of hate: hopeless, with no way out. It was time to turn to God.

I have always believed in God...that tiny, glowing ember of faith was never extinguished, and I am truly thankful for that. I sometimes wandered away from God's love, getting tangled in all of life's trappings, but I still believed. During the good times, I connected with a group of wonderful Christians at my company. They helped me awaken to the reality of Christ. But now this was a true test of what I believed. I was having a hard time seeing God's love through the anger and hatred I was feeling. God is love; He is peace; He is hope. I knew I had to change the way I felt before anything good was going to come of this situation.

I was so caught up in "me" and my frustrations that I ignored John also agonizing over the demands placed upon him. I got along with him at one time; I began to realize that person was still there. I was fairly certain John is not Christian, but I decided to focus my Christian prayers on him. I prayed for John: that

I should not have anger toward him; that I knew he was also put in a position for which he was not suited. I prayed that his boss would not exploit their cultural traditions and would become more reasonable. I did not pray for my situation; I put John's plight before mine. I started to feel more at peace, and it helped take my mind off my own struggles. It helped to see something from another's perspective.

About two weeks later, I heard that John had gotten a job offer from another company. It was in a different state, which made his wife happy. Their daughter was in college there, and they had hoped to move closer to her. John was clearly elated: finally, something good was happening in his life. I could sense he no longer felt trapped; that he now had hope. Soon, the roles of our team began to change. It appeared someone realized putting people into jobs for which they are not suited was having negative results overall.

Then the biggest change happened: the team I had wanted to get into for months finally had an opening. The team leader had wanted me on his team for several years, but with the restructuring, it wasn't possible. The darkness and frustration were starting to fade; I could feel a heavy burden being lifted from my shoulders. I cannot express that feeling of relief, but that is what hope feels like.

It was obvious this had God written all over it. Only God could make all these events happen. It was a great lesson for me. I learned that God wants us to take on someone else's struggles. I learned that we are all children of God, even if we have different beliefs. Because we are His hands and feet, we need to shine that light sometimes where there is none. All it takes is for one believer to accept His love so that many can benefit. And the greatest lesson: nothing is too big for God.

Dave Patti

Chapter 29

God's Love and Blessings Abound

"It seemed every doctor visit had one bad report after another. Once again, by the power of the Holy Spirit, I was able to rise above the circumstances, ignore the negative reports and persevere."

I believe that a God Bump is a time in your life when something happens that you may or may not be expecting or even believe could happen. It is something that only can be explained as the work of a Holy God – A God filled with love and a desire to do good for those who love Him. (Romans 8:28)

God Bumps in my life are numerous, likely many that I didn't realize were God Bumps at the time or since, but times when the hand of God moved on my behalf and made my life ultimately better.

As a young, newly married woman of 22, I desperately wanted a baby. Being a mother was what I had dreamed of, and I just knew it was to be part of God's plan for my life. When the doctor's report came back that I would most likely never be able to carry a baby full-term, my response surprised even me. At that time, I had not yet been taught that faith works (Hebrews 11:1-6); I did not yet understand that the power of life and death is in the tongue (Proverbs 18:21); nor did I realize that where the mind goes the man follows (Proverbs 23:7). Miraculously in that moment in the doctor's office, with my husband by my side, I did not accept that report. I'm sure the doctor thought that I was in extreme denial at the news, as my reaction was unemotional. I truly just didn't receive the report. The Holy Spirit of God rose inside me, and I just knew that I most certainly would become a biological mother someday.

More than a year passed, and I continued to battle a life-threatening autoimmune disease. There were bad days and not-so-bad days, as my case was considered severe with no known cause or cure. My struggle was real, but my belief for a better day was also real. Then it happened, the news we had been hoping for: I was in remission!

After nearly 10 years of suffering, I hit a lull in the symptoms and was told that if I wanted to become pregnant, now would be the time. I conceived that month, in fact, the day of conception was Mother's Day 1990. God is so faithful! I was elated! My husband was nervous and concerned. The medical world was cautiously optimistic, because it was clear that conception was the easy part. Maintaining this pregnancy through the 40 weeks was going to be the real miracle. We needed a God Bump.

My hope of having a natural childbirth experience was shattered because my pregnancy was labeled high risk. I had a team of five obstetric specialists overseeing me and my baby; no sweet midwife in sight as I had hoped. Ultrasounds were routine practice during my numerous exams, making learning the gender a constant temptation. Plus, you needed to know the gender if you wanted to stock up on diapers because they were then sold in gender-specific packages. We gave in and were thrilled to learn that we were expecting a baby boy!

The pregnancy was rough. I worked full-time, was extremely tired all the time and had trouble gaining weight. The weight gain, or lack of it, was extremely problematic as I was underweight going into the pregnancy. It seemed every doctor visit had one bad report after another. Once again, by the power of the Holy Spirit, I was able to rise above the circumstances, ignore the negative reports and persevere. My co-workers said I looked like people they'd only seen on television: suffering from starvation with their thin bodies and extended stomachs. I only gained 10 pounds during the entire pregnancy, which seemed a miracle at the time. Every pound added was celebrated. This journey was certainly a walk of faith, but in the end, after an extremely difficult labor and delivery, including the use of forceps and lots of trauma, we were blessed beyond measure! We welcomed our sweet, 9 lb., 3 oz. baby boy into this world and into our hearts forever.

I praise Jesus for the God Bumps that gave me the greatest gift imaginable. My story doesn't even end there. I am happy to report that I went on to have four more full-term pregnancies and four more beautiful baby boys! Thank you, Father, for your blessings that you promised will chase us down! (Deuteronomy 28:2) As a wonderful bonus, we went to Ukraine and adopted a sibling group of three. Another God Bump! God's love and blessings abound! Being a healthy mother of eight amazing children is a joy, and I praise the Lord for each of the children that confirm every day that I am indeed blessed! (Proverbs 31:28)

Jackie Suecting

Chapter 30

God Never Gave Up on Me

"I would get this feeling of being called back to God, and I kept turning away from Him – until a doctor visit changed everything."

I am sure there are many ways we get a God Bump, but for me it's when I get a chill or a feeling of great happiness. Sometimes it's a beautiful hymn that speaks to me. Other times it's just when I am walking down the road and am suddenly filled with His spirit.

I had a long journey to God. I grew up in a Methodist church. For some reason when I was 17, our family just stopped going. I went on to college, got married, and was busy raising a family. But it was not until I was 35 that I felt something was missing in my life. I started searching for a church that I was comfortable joining. I didn't find what I was looking for at that time and turned away. This happened three more times over the years. I would get this feeling of being called back to God, and I kept turning away from Him – until a doctor visit changed everything.

I was diagnosed with malignant melanoma, and I was so scared! I turned back to God just before my surgery and asked him to guide the doctors to remove all of the

140

cancer and heal me. I promised the Lord to never turn away from him again. It has been seven years, and I am doing well. I am so happy that I found my Redeemer and brought Him back into my life.

After being away from God all that time, I had a lot of catching up to do, reading my Bible and learning to pray again. After a few years in church, our pastor introduced us to "Pray and Watch" a daily devotional to pray for our neighbors who did not know Jesus. I started off doing this daily on my walks, but I wasn't consistent, so it went somewhat by the wayside.

One day I was visiting another church where the pastor also happened to be introducing the "Pray and Watch" devotional, when I was hit hard by a God Bump. I got chills all over my body as I listened to this pastor. I knew then that God was telling me to pray to Him more, that He wanted to know me better. And that by doing this, I might be able to help someone else experience His presence.

It's still a struggle at times, but thankfully I keep finding my way back to Him. Now I know God never gives up on me, even when I sometimes lose my way.

Peggy Wood

Chapter 31

God's Got This

"We looked at each other, hugged, and then tears started. We were so grateful. 'God protected us! Thank you, Jesus! Thank you, God!'"

To me, God Bumps happen when I get a feeling of being touched internally by something you know was not of this world but of the Heavenly world: A good feeling - a feeling of amazement. It's knowing there's only one source of that feeling, and that is God.

We had been driving all day. We had watched the sky in the southwest turn from a pretty blue to an awful, dark, and stormy-looking sky. It looked like we would be driving smack dab into the center of that dark mess. We had just crossed the border into Colorado.

I always say a prayer when we leave on extended driving trips. "Father God in Heaven, please watch over us and protect us as we make another long trip in our car. Put that dome of protection over us and keep us safe as we continue on our journey home. In Jesus' name, Amen." Sometimes I have to say another, just as a shot of encouragement from our Father. This was one of those times.

It was finally my turn to drive. We pulled over and I took over the wheel. The sky had gotten even darker, an eerie sense of dread hung heavy in our car. I repeated my traveling protection prayer to myself.

It had started to rain as we exited the Interstate, getting closer to home. I told my husband, Virgil, "Here it comes." We could see the horrible rain clouds ahead of us with the sun peeking through some areas. Then we saw them - the white sheet clouds that meant there was hail in this storm. "Steady, girl," I said to myself. "You got this."

As we turned south, it started raining more steadily. My hands tightened around the steering wheel, gripping it firmer. I glanced over at Virgil. He seemed only slightly concerned. My rock. I smiled. I can always count on him and his calmness. "We'll be okay. Just be careful," he said. I slowed down because it was starting to rain harder. The wipers were doing their job of keeping our view clear. Within a couple of minutes though, it was getting heavier, and I had to slow down even more.

Then we heard it: the dreaded thunk. It was hail; first one thunk, then another, then another, and another, and another, until we couldn't hear each other talk without shouting. We were creeping along the highway going south of Brush. I had to turn the headlights on because it was so dark out even though the time of day shouldn't have warranted it. We could see hail bouncing off the road in front of us. I had slowed down to maybe 15-20 mph. "The car is going to be nothing but a pitted mess,"

I shouted. Virgil agreed. There was no doubt we were going to be making another insurance claim. We had claimed our camper the year before because of a hailstorm. Our insurance had totaled it, and we knew our rates would go up with this claim. They could drop us altogether.

We drove a few miles, but it felt like we'd been driving forever. "Should we turn around?" I shouted. "Surely it's got to be over us by now, so it would be closer to the back end of the storm than the front end. Besides, isn't there an overpass back a few miles we could wait under?"

"Yup, I think you're right," he shouted. "Let's turn around."

I made a three-point turn in the middle of the highway. I thanked God there was no traffic coming when we made that turn. We were driving totally by faith and trust.

Going back north was just as bad. It hadn't let up at all. We were still creeping along with the hail piling up on the roadsides. It looked like snowdrifts. The hail hit the hood with a "thunk," while some smashed into ice chunks as they hit. We continued to shout at each other to be heard over the loudness of the storm.

In what seemed like an eternity, we finally made it back to town. Even there, it was difficult to see the turns we needed to make to get to the overpass. Once we got there, I pulled to the side of the road under the overpass, feeling some semblance of safety. Soon, the hail let up, but it was still raining. The quiet after the storm was deafening.

We sat in the car a moment, getting our wits about us. We couldn't believe what we had just gone through. I was upset because of the damage that was surely done to our new-to-us 2012 Copperhead Dodge Avenger. I liked that car a lot. But it was time to face the music and see what damage had been done. We both were very curious, and a little scared.

Virgil got out and started to examine the damage. It was still raining but we were under the overpass so we weren't getting wet. I watched him as he was looking at the car. I could see by the expression on his face he was puzzled. A look of disbelief maybe? He had circled the car looking it over as he went and opened his door. "You're not going to believe this but there's not one dent or ping anywhere! After seeing the hail hit like it did, I was positive there would be SOME damage!" "WHAT?!" I exclaimed. He repeated, "There's no damage! I didn't see any dents!"

He climbed in the car and was quiet for a minute, letting it sink in. We both were dumbfounded. We looked at each other, hugged, and then tears started. We were so grateful. "God protected us! Thank you, Jesus! Thank you, God!" I yelled. We were safe; we didn't have to call our insurance company; and we didn't have to get the car fixed. What we did have was a testimony to share with anyone who'd listen, and our faith in God strengthened.

Then I realized something. When I said to myself, "Steady girl, you got this." I should've known better. I didn't have this – God had this all along. What a wonderfully amazing trip home!

Kate Bragg

Chapter 32

The Tree, the Card, and the Magnet

"In this life, we will never understand why things happen. But our Creator reassures us that death is not the end, that we will join Him in eternal life."

I have experienced many goose bumps in my 70 plus years. They have made my skin crawl and my heart pound either from joy or fear. God Bumps, however, are special signs to show we are not alone, and that our Creator knows our pain and longs to comfort. God Bumps go straight to our hearts and souls, fill us with awe and give our minds peace. They always appear in His perfect timing.

My experience with God Bumps revolves around our first grandchild, Cody Robert, the light of our lives. He turned 14 the summer he helped us plant a row of juniper trees in our yard. One morning while my husband tended to chores, I found the spade and started on the trees. The ground was harder than I thought. I had only dug four holes when I heard Cody call out.

"I can dig those holes, Grandma," he said. Cody was

spending the day with us, and I was grateful for his help. I stood for a moment, looking at his bright face and his thin arms. I wondered if he had the strength to spade the tough sod, but he did just fine. In a short time, the dozen trees were planted and looked beautiful. I was grateful for Cody's help and thought of him every time I looked at them.

Ten years passed, the branches filled out and the trees grew strong – except for one in the middle that stayed shorter than the rest. It only had two or three branches, and they were withered green on the edges. A few summers it had shown improvement, but now the branches were dry and brittle. Even with extra watering, it refused to flourish. It was May, and I decided to get rid of that tree this year. It hadn't flourished in 10 years; it was time for it to go.

That month, our dear Cody lost his life in a terrible accident near his home. We lived those awful weeks following the funeral in a surreal world. Full hearts ran on empty. Where was God? How could He have allowed this to happen to this gentle, kind young man? He was only 24! Everything in our lives changed.

A few weeks later, I walked out to the garden, passing the tree I kept meaning to destroy but never found the right time. Touching the lifeless branches, I prayed. "God, if you can raise our dead bodies, you can bring this tree to life! Please bring it back to life!" I was angry with God. I didn't really expect anything to happen.

Three weeks later, I walked past that tree, and I noticed a branch with a spot of green! When I saw it, I felt a bomb of goose bumps, or should I say God Bumps, surge through me. It was awesome! During the next several weeks, the branch produced more green. Then other branches joined. God had answered my prayer. But that was just the first God Bump sent my way after Cody died.

One morning I returned from a walk and noticed a magnet had fallen from the refrigerator. I gasped when I saw it lying on the floor. On it was printed my favorite Bible verse: "Trust in the Lord with all your heart," Proverbs 3:5. I have many magnets, but only this one fell. God Bumps!

I have a wood sign business where I create my own signs and take orders for others. A stencil order came a few days after the magnet incident. The company sent a business card with the order. I was shocked when I turned it over and read the back. There was another of my favorite Bible verses, "I can do all things through Christ which strengthens me," Philippians 4:13. I had stenciled that verse many times on my own sign creations. God Bumps!

I believe God answered my prayers, in His time, in His way. Two years later, the short tree is thick with lacy growth on one side. It may never fill out any more than it has or get taller, but it doesn't matter. That shrub was God's instrument when we needed comfort, just as the magnet and the card were.

In this life, we will never understand why things happen. But our Creator reassures us that death is not the end, that we will join him in eternal life. Yes, everything in our lives changed when we lost Cody, but one thing stayed constant: God's love. He showed His presence and comforted us in awesome and mysterious ways. We know we will see our precious Cody Robert again! I have the God Bumps to prove it.

Marylyn Diebold

Chapter 33

A Picture is Worth a Thousand Words

"I can't begin to count the holy images
that I've seen in my life. But I do know,
they are signs from God that He is with us,
and that He wants us to experience His love."

Some people feel God Bumps coursing through their bodies. Some people feel them coming out from their souls. Others feel them as if they're coming down from above. I can say I've actually seen them!

Since I was young, I've seen many visions, or what I call "holy images." I don't know why they appear to me, and there doesn't seem to be a reason for them to appear. I haven't shared these happenings with many people because I didn't want them to think I was crazy. I had a rather hard life as a child, so maybe the Good Lord gave me this gift to calm my soul. But they are real, and whenever I see one, I am filled with an overwhelming feeling of peace.

I've seen the face of Jesus in the snow, and St. Michael, the archangel, once appeared to me in the sky when I was praying. When we were younger, my husband was stationed in Germany in the military. Once, I was in a church and saw a statue of the Blessed Mother grow from a child to an adult. We traveled all over, and I described my sightings to several priests. They were not surprised and were interested in what I had seen.

In 2016, my daughter Linda and family were planning to be at my place to celebrate Christmas. The weather forecast was for heavy snow for Christmas Day, so we decided to celebrate Christmas Eve as they live 45 miles from me. When I closed the patio blinds the night before, I could see three-four feet of snow already piled up. It was impossible to walk in the backyard or even to get out the patio door.

When Linda's family arrived on Christmas Eve morning, I was getting food ready and asked my 19-year-old granddaughter, Jackie, to open the blinds. As the sun came pouring in, she turned to me and said, "Grandma you have an angel in your backyard." Without looking, I told her it was probably the statue of the Blessed Mother she saw. She insisted, "No, Grandma, there is an angel."

We all piled into the sunroom, and just couldn't believe what was before our eyes: a beautiful eight-foot angel in the evergreen tree. Linda opened the door slightly, stuck her arm out, and took a picture with her phone. I said, "It wasn't there the night before when I closed the blinds. This is a miracle." That angel did a good job giving us God Bumps that day! I later showed the picture to my priest. "That could only happen at Phyllis's house," he said.

Just this spring when my daughter Linda was taking a picture of a rainbow at our farm, lightning struck. At that moment, an image of the Blessed Mother appeared to be reflected on the metal grain bin, and we were able to get a photo of it. God Bump!

I can't begin to count the holy images that I've seen in my life. But I do know, they are signs from God that He is with us, and that He wants us to experience His love. Peace be with you.

Phyllis Lentz

Thank You!

A huge thank you goes out to all who shared their God Bumps stories. This book of hope would be impossible without each of your stories. Your generosity will give others hope and encourage them to never give up.

Philippians 4:13
I can do all things through Him who strengthens me.

For all readers of *God Bumps*

These stories may not be yours, but they are your neighbors, your friends, and others.

I pray that you will offer your lonely silence and your secret grief to God and trust He will turn all of it into God Bumps. After All, He is the listener of listeners.

So without hurry any distraction, be silent, and then talk to Him: He, who never a word is not heard…His timing is perfect.

Romans 8:28
And we know that God causes all things to work together for good to those who love God, to those who are called according to His purpose.

www.ingramcontent.com/pod-product-compliance
Lightning Source LLC
Chambersburg PA
CBHW051523120626
46551CB00012B/1048